How to Beat Satan and Free Your Family

A Parent's Guide for Spiritual Warfare

Kathleen Myers

COPYRIGHT

Copyright © 2025 Kathleen Myers

Published by

All rights reserved. No part of this book may be reproduced or transmitted in any form or by any means, electronic or mechanical, including photocopying, recording, or by any information storage and retrieval system, without written permission from the publisher and author.

DEDICATION

I dedicate this book to all parents and grandparents who are concerned about the spiritual well-being of their children. If you are struggling because you are not sure what to do. "Fear not, God is with you." As you and your family move from war to peace and from darkness to light, I will be praying for you.

I dedicate this book to Terry, my husband. He lived every day serving, loving, helping, and guiding others. He showed them how to receive God's love, to turn to Jesus for compassion and wisdom, and to the Holy Spirit for guidance. Even though Terry is with Jesus, his ministry to others is ongoing. Today, those who lived in despair are not, those who lived in fear are not, those who lived in addiction are not, and those who lived in disbelief are not. In their freedom, others are now free.

Index

INTRODUCTION 7

CHAPTER 1

God Sees Your Children 10

God Thinks Children are Special 12

God's Expectations for Your Children 14

Jesus Loves Your Child 16

CHAPTER 2

Divine Authority Given to Parents 18

Parents Protect Their Children from Demons 20

CHAPTER 3

Children Need Protection and Care 24

Children Need Guidance in Their Faith 26

Parents Help Children Stay Closer to God 30

CHAPTER 4

Explanation of Demons 33

Demons Attack Children and Teens 37

CHAPTER 5

The Bible and Spiritual Warfare 44

Spiritual Warfare 50

Parents Must Be Alert and Trained 54

Spiritual Warfare Weapons God Gave Parents 58

The Armor of God 61

Parents Do Spiritual Warfare 66

CHAPTER 6

Demonic Footholds 72

Demonic Strongholds 74

Open Doors 76

Signs of Demonic Intrusion 79

Ways to Make Demons Leave 84

Demons Response When You Pray to God 87

CHAPTER 7

Deliverance Ministry 89

Spiritual Warfare Through the Bible and Prayer 94

Spiritual Warfare for Your Family 98

Pray Guidance and Protection over Yourself and Your Family
.... 105

CHAPTER 8

Cleanse Your Home of Demonic Influence 109

Bless Your Home 114

Cleanse Your Property of Demonic Influence 124

Prayers for Protection Over Your Property 126
Consecrate Your Home and Property to God 128
Spiritual Warfare Scriptures 130

CHAPTER 9

Baptism and Your Children 134
Baptizing Infants 139
Baptizing Young Children 143
Baptizing of Teens 146
Baptism by the Holy Spirit 151

INTRODUCTION

My life has been centered on God and Jesus for as long as I can remember. I knew He was there, but did not really understand how the Trinity, God the Father, God the Son, and God the Holy Spirit work together as One. When I understood who God really is, I learned that He always has a better way and that He walks the walk with me daily. That is when everything changed.

In my early twenties, I became a member of the Episcopal Church. In my mid-twenties, I went to work for an Episcopal Church as a lay professional. Over the next 20 years, I became a Director of Christian Education, a Christian Curriculum writer for children and young people, a Christian Education Teacher for Church volunteers, and a member of a multi-denominational Exorcism Team. As God would have it, He placed me in several different churches across the country as a Christian Education Director, a Director of Lay Ministry, a Co-Director and co-author of a The Bishop School of Lay Ministry, a Seminarian Christian Education supervisor, a Christian education and goal setting consultant for leadership and teachers in various denominations around the country, a Pastural Counselor and an author of Christian Children books. I had no formal education in Christian Education, Training Teachers to Teach, Pastoral Counseling, Theology, Liturgy, Public Speaking, Goal Setting, writing Curriculum and Books. But God had a plan for me.

For the next 20 years, God sent me to the philanthropic and business world. He provided me with an opportunity to minister to others in a different setting. During this time, God gave me ample opportunity to learn about leadership, budgets, goal setting, teaching, counseling, negotiating, raising money, and much more. Over these years, I became the president of a national software corporation, a retail business owner, a cattle rancher, a potbelly pig breeder, an author, and the working president of a philanthropic organization. Amazing, huh? There is no way this could have happened without direction from God and His divine intervention. God had another plan for me. Even though I did not have the correct degrees and the knowledge to follow these callings from God, God found a way.

Over my life, I have learned God walks with us, guides us, and always provides what we need to follow His plan for our lives. If you are willing to listen and to follow Him, God will also direct you. He will give you what you need to do His work in your family and in the world.

Today, I am a mother of 6, grandmother of 1, and great-grandmother of 2. I have learned from all of this living = anything is possible. If you have faith in God and get out of His way, He will lead you, and miracles will happen. Things you thought were never possible are possible, and skills you thought you never had become real. So, here I sit as a sample of what God can do if you just let Him.

Everything I have ever done in my life prepared me for my next step, even if I did not know what my next step would be. In my early fifties, I became a volunteer at Antioch Church, Waco. I have been a missionary board member in charge of the missionary houses, a Life Group Leader, an usher, and a coordinator for several Church teaching events. Currently, I am a Life Group Leader, a Prophet Prayer Team Coach, a Sunday morning Intercessor, a Mentor for women, and most importantly to me, a Deliverance Minister. I can now add to this list the author of "How to Defeat Satan at His Own Game", which was written so that you can enter spiritual warfare with confidence, knowledge, and skill.

My second book, "How to Beat Satan and Free Your Family – A Parent's Guide for Spiritual Warfare" provides you with knowledge and strategies for guiding and protecting your children, from infancy through their teen years. With the help of Jesus and the Holy Spirit, you can defeat Satan and save your children from demonic attack. It will help you enable your children to have a closer relationship with God and with you; as well as identify Satanic influences and how demons can be defeated. This defeat can mean freedom for those you love, so they can become who God means for them to be. Jesus gave us authority, as His disciples, to conquer Satan and to help those who are in demonic bondage. You, as a believer in Christ, can defeat Satan and his demons through the love of God, the powerful name of Jesus Christ, and the wisdom and guidance of the Holy Spirit. God is on our side.

Read, study, and prepare yourself, as you turn to God for direction. Though His infinite wisdom and great love for you and your family, He will give you all of the tools we need to take on Satan's demons and win the war without fear.

I will be praying for you, as you move forward in your walk with God. May He direct and protect you and those you love. "Fear not for I am with you always, even until the end of the age." *(Matthew 8:20)*.

CHAPTER 1
God Sees Your Children

In the Old Testament, God is portrayed as caring for and blessing children. They are a heritage and reward from Him. God emphasizes the importance of parents nurturing, guiding, and teaching their children His ways and laws. The Old Testament emphasizes the responsibility of parents as they train their children in the correct way, ensuring they will grow into responsible and faithful individuals.

Children as a Heritage and Blessing

The Bible frequently portrays children as a gift from God, emphasizing their value and significance in families and their importance to the community.

"Behold, children are a heritage from the LORD, the fruit of the womb a reward. Like arrows in the hand of a warrior are the children of one's youth. Blessed is the man who fills his quiver with them! He shall not be put to shame when he speaks with his enemies in the gate." *(Psalm 127:3-5).*

"All your children shall be taught by the LORD, and great shall be the peace of your children." *(Isaiah 54:13).*

"Before I formed you in the womb I knew you, and before you were born I consecrated you; I appointed you a prophet to the nations." *(Jeremiah 1:5).*

God's Plan for Children

God commands Adam and Eve to "Be fruitful and multiply," indicating that children are integral to His original plan for humanity. This verse highlights the importance of families and the continuation of God's covenant across generations.

God blessed them and said to them, "Be fruitful and increase in number; fill the earth and subdue it. Rule over the fish in the sea and the birds in the sky and over every living creature that moves on the ground." *(Genesis 1:28)*.

"Start children off on the way they should go, and even when they are old they will not turn from it." *(Proverbs 22:6)*.

"Children are a heritage from the Lord, offspring a reward from Him. Like arrows in the hands of a warrior are children born in one's youth. Blessed is the man who quiver is full of them. They will not be put to share when they contend with their opponents in court." *(Psalm 127:3-5)*.

God's Love and Care for Children

While not clearly stated in every verse, the Old Testament tells you about God's love and care for children. He directs parents to nurture and guide them. By doing this, God promises blessings for children who honor their parents.

"Fathers, do not exasperate your children; instead, bring them up in the training and instruction of the Lord." *(Ephesians 6:4)*.

"These commandments that I give you today are to be on your hearts. Impress them on your children. Talk about them when you sit at home and when you walk along the road, when you lie down, and when you get up." *(Deuteronomy 6:6-9)*.

"Discipline your children, and they will give you peace; they will bring you the delights you desire." *(Proverbs 29:17)*.

God Thinks Children are Special

Children are gifts from God, not something to be earned or possessed. God thinks every child is special and is deeply loved by Him. The Bible emphasizes the unique value of every child and affirms their important role in God's plan. It states that "children are a heritage from the Lord, the fruit of the womb a reward". *(Psalm 127:3).*

- God made each child unique and has great plans for them.

    "For I know the plans I have for you, declares the Lord, plans to prosper you and not to harm you, plans to give you hope and a future" *(Jeremiah 29:11).*

- God loves every child.

    His love is not dependent on their behavior, their achievements, or their obedience. He loves His children no matter what they say or do. "For I am convinced that neither death nor life, neither angels or demons, neither the present not the future, not any powers, neither height not depth, not anything else in all creation, will be able to separate us from the love of God that is Christ Jesus our Lord." *(Romans 8:38-39).*

- God is with every child.

    Even when a child feels afraid, they can be confident that God is always with them. They are always safe because God is near. "Have I not commanded you? Be strong and courageous. Do not be afraid; do not be discouraged, for the Lord your God will be with you wherever you go." *(Joshua 1:9).*

- God sent Jesus for every child to love and cherish them.

    There is no child who does not deserve the love and sacrifice of Jesus. "For God so loved the world that He gave

His one and only Son, that whoever believes in Him shall not perish but have eternal life." *(John 3:16)*.

- Jesus loves your children

    Children can learn to love people just like Jesus. He loves all of us, especially our children. Due to His great love and compassion, He lives within each child, who can learn to give this same gift of love to everyone they meet. "My command is this: Love each other as I have loved you." *(John 15:12)*.

God's Expectations for Your Children

God expects all of His children to be loving, kind, forgiving, faithful, and to treat others with compassion. You are called to teach them to be obedient, to encourage them to stay close to God, and to love Him with all their heart, soul, and strength. Ultimately, God desires your child to be like Christ and to live in a way that reflects His love and grace.

Living a Life of Love and Compassion

God expects His children to love everyone, even their enemies, and to treat them with love, kindness, and compassion.

Forgiveness

God expects children to forgive others and to forgive themselves.

Serving Others

God expects His children to be actively involved in serving others and making a positive impact in the world.

Obedience to Parents

God expects children to be obedient to their parents, realizing that this obedience pleases God.

Humility

God expects His children to be humble, acknowledging their dependence on Him, and to know that their strength and wisdom come from Him.

Living a Holy Life

God expects His children to strive for holiness - meaning to be set apart and to live in a way that honors Him. He wants His children to live in a way that reflects the character and teachings of Jesus Christ.

Developing Faith

God expects His children to learn about their faith, understand its teachings, and develop a personal relationship with God.

Worship and Prayer

God expects His children to participate in worship and prayer, which can help them deepen their connection with Him.

Jesus Loves Your Child

In the New Testament, God views children as a precious blessing and a gift. They are described as a heritage and a reward from Him. This shows their great value and importance to God. Jesus emphasized they hold a special place in God's Kingdom. He demonstrated His love for children by inviting them closer to Him and by blessing them. He taught that those who enter the Kingdom of God need to become like a little child's heart: one that is innocent, trusting, loving, and faithful.

God lives within you and is a spiritual reality. The Holy Spirit transforms you from within. When your child follows Jesus, it is not just a future event; it is a present experience. Jesus helps your child reach their full potential as a person and as a parent.

Children and the Kingdom of God

Jesus' teachings and interactions emphasize the importance of your child. He used children as examples of humility, and that you should strive to be as humble. He emphasizes that, in God's eyes, your child is valuable and that children play an important role in God's plan.

Jesus said that children are a model for entering the Kingdom of God, pointing out the need for childlike humility, love, and receptiveness. He taught that the kingdom of God belongs to those who are like children. Jesus stresses the need for you to help your child show this same simplicity of trust, faith. love, and humility.

Because Jesus cares deeply for your children, He expresses His love, guidance, and protection for them. You as a parent, are expected to love, guide, and protect your child. You must treat your child as God treats you, with love, care, and compassion.

Jesus often uses children as examples of humility and faith, encouraging adults to be like them in their simplicity and trust in God.

"People were bringing children to Jesus so he could touch them, and his disciples rebuked them. But when Jesus saw this, he was indignant and said to them, 'Let the children come to me; do not hinder them, for the kingdom of God belongs to those who are like these children." *(Mark 10:13-16).*

"Jesus took a child in his arms, placed his hands on him and blessed him. Then he said, 'Whoever welcomes one such child in my name welcomes me; and whoever welcomes me, welcomes not me but the one who sent me." *(Mark 9:36-37).*

"Let the little children come to me, and do not hinder them, for the kingdom of God belongs to such as these. Truly I tell you, anyone who will not receive the kingdom of God like a little child will never enter it." *(Luke 18:16-17).*

"Truly I tell you, unless you turn and become like little children, you will never enter the kingdom of heaven. Whoever humbles himself like this little child is the greatest in the kingdom of heaven." *(Matthew 18:3-4).*

"See that you do not despise one of these little ones, for I say to you that their angels in heaven continually see the face of My Father who is in heaven.": *(Matthew 18:10).*

CHAPTER 2

Divine Authority Given to Parents

God has a special connection with you as a parent. He emphasizes your role in raising your children in faith and obedience to God. He also expects you to guide and train your children in His word, so they can better understand the relationship He has with them and with you. The fifth commandment, "Honor your father and your mother," *(Exodus 12:20)* highlights the importance of respect and obedience to parents, as well as your responsibility and authority to train your children in God's ways. *(Proverbs 22:6, Colossians 3:20)*.

God has given you authority over your children. You are accountable to God for how you exercise it, including raising, educating, and guiding your children in a way that aligns with God's will. And, for children, this emphasizes the importance of honoring parents and obeying them. "Children, obey your parents in the Lord, for this is right." *(Ephesians 6:1)*.

God expects a relationship between you and your child. Each of you play a different role. Yours is to diligently teach your children about Him and His ways, including nurturing, disciplining, promoting obedience, instilling respect, praying, leading by example, and making a commitment to God's teachings. *(Deuteronomy 6:4-9, Ephesians 6:4, Proverbs 22:6)*.

Your Role with Your Children

- You are called to teach your children about God and His ways.

- You are called to significantly influence your child's understanding of God and their faith.

- You are called to set an example by modeling God's character and teachings.

- You are called, through love and compassion, to teach your children to be obedient to you and to God.
- You are called to provide an atmosphere in your home that allows your family to build a relationship with God.
- You are called to guide your children through various stages of life, helping your child develop a strong faith and moral compass.

There can be situations where your child's faith and your beliefs may conflict. This requires you to keep a balanced approach, as you and your children pursue God's truth and wisdom together.

Even though you strive to follow God's principles, you are not perfect and will make mistakes. To help remedy your mistakes, repent and ask your child to forgive you. It is important for you to receive your child's forgiveness, as well as encourage your child to seek and receive God's guidance. In other words, you can model Christ for your child in this and all situations.

"Honor your father and your mother, that your days may be long in the land that the Lord your God is giving you". *(Proverbs 22:6)*.

"Children, obey your parents in the Lord, for this is right. Honor your father and mother"—which is the first commandment with a promise— "so that it may go well with you and that you may enjoy long life on the earth." Fathers, do not exasperate your children; instead, bring them up in the training and instruction of the Lord." *(Ephesians 6:1-4)*.

Parents Protect Their Children from Demons

As a parent who loves the Lord and loves your child, you will do everything possible to protect your child from any danger, including evil. You are responsible for helping your child recognize the deceptive and destructive forces of evil surrounding them. Demons often disguise themselves as harmless or even good, as they seek to take ground from you and your child. It can sometimes be difficult to determine what is good and what is not, because Satan and his demons lie constantly. Their purpose is to blind you to what is good, to kill, steal, and destroy the good within you, and to steal souls from God.

Satan has always hated children. Scripture reveals the slaughter of infants in Pharaoh's Egypt and Herod's Bethlehem. Many times, demonic powers oppose Jesus, and "babies are caught in the crossfire." Through political plots and military conquests, Pharaoh and Herod used their armies to rip babies from pregnant mothers' wombs *(Amos 1:13)*. Today, it seems they try to destroy children by destroying families through any means available.

There is a spiritual war against children. They are always caught in the crossfire and harmed. Children are victims of a larger conflict in which they have no say, influence, or responsibility. This was true when primitive peoples thought slaying children would appease the gods. It happened during wars that produced burning homes, sacked villages, and murdered people, including children. Today, children are killed by unstable, violent people who carry weapons into schools, colleges, churches, businesses, abortion clinics, rallies, and other events, all with the intent to kill and destroy.

Satan and his demons hate children because they symbolize God's blessing, expression of faith, and the future hope of humanity. Demons like to destroy the most vulnerable among us, the children. They hinder God's purposes for your child and for all humanity.

The Shift in Perspective

There is a war going on against your child; you play a critical role in it. As a faithful and loving parent, you are called to move forward and protect your child from evil, including demonic attacks. This may cause a shift in your perspective. It is unwise to be naïve and ignore the problem. Should you do this, it will not be long before trouble and despair appear for your family.

Do not think this war is easy. Demons have preyed on adults and children since the Garden of Eden. Their goal is to steal souls from God and cause havoc and pain in the world. When you engage in this demonic battle, it is essential to remember you are not alone—God the Father, the Son, and the Holy Spirit all fight alongside you.

Viewing your parenting through the lens of spiritual warfare helps you reorganize your work in at least five important ways.

A Shift in Society

In our society today, children are increasingly seen as miniature adults—a significant societal shift. As a parent, you may have a limited understanding of childhood as a distinct, formative period of life. This change affects parenting styles and social expectations.

Today, parents often approach child-rearing with the same bold sense of independence and individuality they apply to other life projects. Some see children as commodities meant to make them happy, boost their egos, or earn praise for any success. Many have children, expecting that they will improve their lives. Because of this, some parents struggle when challenges arise—such as when children misbehave in public, refuse to stay in bed, or disobey instructions. Anger often results from incorrect expectations that children will always obey immediately.

Some parents do not understand why their children disobey or how to teach obedience. In times like this, it is vital to turn to God for help and recognize that you may be fighting hell for your child. When you understand spiritual warfare is at play, parenting looks different. Knowing it is present helps you enter the fight with love, correction, and kindness. Knowing you wrestle with demons makes disobedience less surprising.

A Shift in Strategy

When spiritual warfare is active, parenting is more complicated than you expected. No single parenting model used today will work perfectly to guide and heal your child. Parenting is often hard. Remember, you may be wrestling with demons. Pray for your children and offer help when needed. View situations through the eyes of love—not anger or frustration.

Satan's message that children are worthless is a lie. Thinking this way only brings grief. Children are everything. They are a child of God. See them as they are meant to be and not how they are acting today. Love your children, even when they make a terrible mistake. You are their parent. Make them the center of your world.

In spiritual warfare, you learn the enemy has many ways to wreak havoc. Demons delight in homes run by children or where parents are uninvolved. These children lack the ability to distinguish right from wrong or recognize their need for a Savior. Your children are gifts and blessings from God *(Psalm 127:3-5)*. They are never mistakes. regardless of their good or bad behavior. Children are not perfect, but they are made by God and are always inherently good.

Sometimes it is hard to understand why children act badly. It is tiring and difficult to deal with misled children. You might question if you will make it through. God is always there to help you. When you do make it, you will feel deep contentment and joy.

Know God fights on your side. It can be hard to fully grasp how much Jesus loves your children—perhaps even more than you do. When Jesus said, "Let the little children come to me," He meant it for now and eternity. He advocates for your children. Scripture speaks of children as the youngest and frailest among us, assuring you God always fights on your side. With God's help, you can face the fight without fear, frustration, or anger. God provides everything your children need to live faithful, happy lives.

CHAPTER 3
Children Need Protection and Care

Protecting children is a core Christian value. The Bible highlights the importance of safeguarding children from harm and exploitation. This includes creating safe environments inside and outside the home, which ensures their physical, emotional, and spiritual well-being.

Biblical Basis for Child Protection

Moral Obligations

The Bible calls on you to care for orphans, widows, and the vulnerable, offering protection and justice.

Preventing Harm

The Bible condemns practices like child abuse, slavery, and exploitation, emphasizing the need to protect your children from harm.

Specific Actions and Practices

Create Safe Environments

Provide your children with a Christ-centered home where they feel loved, valued, and safe.

Encourage Open Communication

Create an environment where your children feel comfortable asking questions and sharing their concerns.

Establish Discipline

Christian discipline is a loving guidance and correction aimed at training your children in righteousness, which leads them to a life of faith. Seek wisdom from God through Bible study and prayer.

Discipline methods should be age-appropriate. Consistency helps children understand expectations and learn from mistakes. Discipline must be administered with grace and forgiveness, just as God disciplines His children with love and compassion. Even in difficult times, trust that God is intimately connected to you and your child.

Set Boundaries

Discuss with your children that boundaries are like fences protecting hearts and guiding interactions. They are not walls to shut others out, but healthy limits ensuring respect, trust, and growth.

Spiritual Nurturing

Providing a safe, loving environment will enable your children to grow in faith and develop a closer relationship with God. Demonstrate your own faith through prayer, scripture, and kindness.

Empowerment

Help your child seek God's love and guidance and develop self-worth vital for long-term well-being.

Children Need Guidance in Their Faith

The Bible emphasizes children's vulnerability and need for guidance and support. You are to teach your children the Bible. The Lord warns that it is a sin not to teach children about faith, repentance, baptism, and the gift of the Holy Spirit. You are to teach your children to pray and obey the Lord's commandments. You are responsible for their spiritual care and well-being.

"Train up a child in the way he should go; even when he is old he will not depart from it." This verse underscores the importance of early and consistent guidance in faith. *(Proverbs 22:6)*.

"These commandments that I give you today are to be on your hearts. Impress them on your children. Talk about them when you sit at home and when you walk along the road, when you lie down and when you get up." This emphasizes the importance of integrating faith into daily life. *(Deuteronomy 6:6-7)*.

As a parent, your primary role is to help your child cultivate a relationship with God and live according to His teachings. This involves trusting in God, seeking His guidance through prayer, and striving to live a life that reflects His love and character. It means honoring God by doing His will in this world. As a godly parent, God promises to bless you for loving your child as God loves you, for teaching your child how to build a relationship with Him, and for modeling the personal relationship you have with God.

God Expects Your Children:

- To honor and obey their parents, as outlined in the Bible. "Children, obey your parents in the Lord, for this is right." Honor your father and mother"—which is the first commandment with a promise—" so that it may go well with you and that you may enjoy long life on the earth." *(Ephesians 6:1-4)*.

- To bring your children up in the training and instruction of the Lord. "Children, obey your parents in everything, for this pleases the Lord. Fathers, do not embitter your children, or they will become discouraged." *(Colossians 3:20-21).*

- To worship God by giving Him praise, honor, and devotion, as seen in expressions of singing, prayer, and thanksgiving, and the act of living one's life as a "living sacrifice." *(Hebrews 12-38).*

- Doing what is right and pleasing to God involves living a life of integrity, justice, and righteousness and aligning your desires and actions with God's will. *(Romans 12:1-2).*

- To learn the importance of serving others and to discover the joy of selfless service in God's kingdom, like Jesus did, "Do nothing out of selfish ambition or vain conceit. Rather, in humility value others above yourselves, not looking to your own interests but each of you to the interests of the others. In your relationships with one another, have the same mindset as Christ Jesus: Who, being in very nature God, did not consider equality with God something to be used to his own advantage; rather, he made himself nothing by taking the very nature of servant, being made in human likeness. And being found in appearance as a man, he humbled himself by becoming obedient to death—even death on a cross!" *(Philippians 2:3-8).*

- To love God as He loves your children, reflecting God's own selfless, compassionate, and enduring love by extending kindness, forgiveness, and a desire for the good of others, particularly fellow believers.

  "I have given them the glory you gave me, so that they may be one as we are one, I in them and you in me—so that they may be brought to complete unity. Then the world will know that you sent me and have loved them even as you *have loved me". (John 17:23).*

- To live your life in agreement with their faith means to love your children, raising them according to biblical principles by modeling godly behavior, teaching them Scripture, praying with and for them, and instilling a love for God and His ways. "Train up a child in the way he should go; even when he is old he will not depart from it," *(Proverbs 22:6).*

- To continue growing and learning in faith, prioritize spiritual practices like reading the Bible and praying, connect with a church community, serve others, and live by God's principles, putting God first in daily choices and future plans.

- Godly children honor, respect, and obey their parents, and serve others. As their parent, It is your responsibility to teach them to love God and others, understand God's Word, and live out their faith in all aspects of their lives. These expectations are not about perfection, but about striving to live a life that reflects God's character and values.

- "I have no greater joy than to hear that my children are walking in the truth." *(3 John 1:4).*

- "Who is the greatest in the kingdom of heaven?" And calling to him a child, he put him in the midst of them and said, "Truly, I say to you, unless you turn and become like children, you will never enter the kingdom of heaven." *(Matthew 18:1-3).*

- "Whoever receives one such child in my name receives me, and whoever receives me, receives not me but him who sent me." *(Mark 9:37).*

- "See that you do not despise one of these little ones. For I tell you that in heaven their angels always see the face of my Father who is in heaven." *(Matthew 18:10).*
- "Fathers, do not provoke your children to anger, but bring them up in the discipline and instruction of the Lord." *(Ephesians 6:4).*

Parents Help Children Stay Closer to God

The idea that children stay close to God or feel a stronger connection to Him is often linked to their innocence, faith, and growing understanding of the world. Children naturally possess faith and innocence, allowing them to accept and grasp spiritual concepts more easily than adults, who may struggle with doubts.

As a parent, nurture your children through prayer, reading the Bible, and church activities. You play an important role in their spiritual growth by guiding, teaching about God's love, and creating a home that promotes faith and love.

Learning and Development

As children develop, they learn about God through stories, teachings, and modeling their parents and other adults.

Connecting Through Nature

Some children may feel a stronger connection to God through nature, experiencing His creation as a way to connect with the divine.

Participate in the Church

By joining the church in prayer and Bible study, your child better understands a relationship with God.

Parental Spiritual Guidance

You play a vital role in nurturing your child's spiritual growth, offering guidance and teaching about God's love. Building a home that fosters faith is important for your family.

Parents Cultivates Faith

Your child builds their relationship with you by seeing your loving faith lived out daily. Encourage your child to express gratitude, serve others, and spend time with fellow Christians.

Building a Relationship with God

- Prayer is a regular part of your family's life—through group prayers, quiet reflection, or simple personal prayers. Praying alongside your child helps them understand prayer's significance and how to connect with God. As you pray, explain God's love to make prayer more meaningful to your child.
- Reading Bible stories to your children, especially while they are young, teach them about God's love, His teachings, and the lives of biblical figures. Use age-appropriate Bibles, apps, or simple stories to capture their interest. Provide older children with their own Bible and discuss how its teachings apply to their lives. Encourage your child to read together as a family. Let your children ask questions and express their thoughts about what they are learning from the Bible.
- Attend church regularly with your children to expose them to the teachings of the faith, worship, and a community of believers. Urge your child to participate in Sunday school, youth groups, or church programs to develop meaningful relationships and learn more about God.
- Show your child how you live your faith through words, actions, and relationships with others. Acknowledge your personal relationship with God.
- Get involved with your child in acts of service in your community. Such as volunteering or donating—so they learn about God's love and compassion for others.
- Regularly express gratitude for God's blessings and provision. This helps your children develop a thankful heart.
- Listening to worship music and singing praise songs can help your children connect with God and build a love for His presence.

- Surrounding your children with positive Christian role models and mentors can help them grow in faith and develop a strong sense of community.
- Exploring nature, whether through walks in the park or visits to a zoo, can help your children appreciate God's power and creativity.
- Allowing your children to engage in playful interactions with God can help them understand His love and presence in a way that is relatable and engaging.

CHAPTER 4
Explanation of Demons

Demons are spiritual beings. They do not have physical bodies. They do not live, grow old, and die like human beings, but exist in a spiritual state. Because of this, they have significant power and influence in the world. They have far less power than God, who rules over them, and at Jesus's name they tremble.

Satan and other fallen angels rejected God's rule. They were cast out of Heaven and are now known on Earth as demons. These demons are fully fallen, desperately evil, and serve the supreme ruler of Hell, Satan. They are evil to the core and seek to harm humanity, including your children.

Demons are under God's judgment. The Bible confirms that Satan will be chained in the abyss for a thousand years (Revelation 20:1-10). The abyss is described as a prison for Satan and demons, as they await their final judgment. After that judgment, they will never again be free to disturb God's creation. "For if God did not spare angels when they sinned, but sent them to hell, putting them in chains of darkness to be held for judgment;" (*2 Peter 2:4*).

Since the fall, demons have sought to kill, steal, and destroy mankind. They want to turn everyone away from God, including your children. They plan to steal souls by opposing God's kingdom, corrupting humanity, and destroying as much of God's creation as possible.

One way they plan on doing this is by attacking your children (*Mark 7:15-20, Luke 9:37-42, Matthew 15:21-28*). They want to destroy God's plan and purpose for you and your children. They try to make your children lose interest in their passions, withdraw from their family, choose "friends" who lead them away from God, and much more. Demons use all means available to separate your children from God. They want the worst for your child and seek to destroy them, so your child cannot fulfill God's purpose. Everything can turn from light to darkness, good to bad, and joy to fear. When this happens, demons influence your child's life in the most destructive way possible. (*Proverbs 16:27-29*).

Mission of Demons

Demons are evil at their core and seek to kill, steal, and destroy as many people as possible by:

Temptation and Deception

Demons can lure you into wrongdoing through deception, temptation, and manipulation.

Chaos and Destruction

Demons' actions cause disruption, harm, and chaos for you, your children, and society.

Opposition to Goodness

Demons want to turn all of mankind away from God. They want to lead you and your children away from Jesus, the Bible, and God's purpose in your life, hindering your spiritual growth and destroying God's plan for you.

Satan and his demons attack adults and children. (*Mark 7:15-20, Luke 9:37-42, Matthew 15:21-28*). They absolutely want the worst for your family. They want to influence your children's interests and passions to the point that they withdraw from the family. Demons can cause your children to choose "friends" who lead them away from God. The closer they get to your children, the more demons interact with them, and the more they try to destroy them. Demons do not want anyone to achieve God's purpose in their life. In some of the most destructive ways possible, demons will lead your children into sin, destruction, and in some cases, death.

Demons accomplish this in two ways:

Demonic oppression is the demonic influence on your children's minds, bodies, and emotions. Demonic oppression symptoms can range from a general lack of motivation and joy to specific behaviors or thoughts that are contrary to God's character. When your children believe in Jesus as their Lord and Savior, are baptized, and receive the Holy Spirit, they can still be oppressed by demons through sin, bad choices, and generational curses.

Demonic Oppression manifests as:

- A lack of interest in spiritual activities
- Difficulty in prayer
- Persistent negative thoughts and emotions.
- Disobedience
- Decline in health and relationship with friends and family.

Demonic Possession can profoundly affect many areas of your children's lives, especially if they are spiritually vulnerable. In severe cases, demons can take over their mind, body, emotions, and soul, turning their lives from light to darkness, good to bad, and joy to fear.

Demonic Possession manifests as:

- Hallucinations, strange behavior, extreme unrest, voice changes, speaking in foreign languages, seizures, and superhuman strength.
- Personality shifts, violence, and self-mutilation are also associated with demonic possession.
- Superhuman strength, physical pain, and a change in voice are among the physical manifestations attributed to demonic possession

If your children are not believers or unbaptized, it is much harder for them to resist evil. But when your children proclaim Jesus as

Lord and are baptized, you can trust in Jesus's power to protect them. With the Holy Spirit dwelling in your children, you have help, guidance, and protection against demonic attacks. "A scoundrel plots evil, and on their lips it is like a scorching fire. A perverse person stirs up conflict, and a gossip separates close friends. A violent person entices their neighbor and leads them down a path that is not good." (*Proverbs 16:27-29*)

Demons Attack Children and Teens

Satan opposes God and everything good, including your children. Children represent the future and are vital to God's plan for growing His kingdom. Satan's goal is to disrupt this plan by influencing children to reject God's teachings and by leading parents to neglect their children's spiritual needs.

Children as a Symbol of God's Kingdom

In Jesus' eyes, children are examples of innocence, purity, and a simple, loving faith. They are the absolute opposite to Satan's nature, the embodiment of evil. Christian theology views children as a blessing and a representation of the future growth of God's kingdom.

Satan's goal is to corrupt and lead children away from God. Because of a child's vulnerability and openness, they are a prime, easy target for demonic influence. Satan is actively trying to disrupt or destroy children, all of whom are precious to God. Because Jesus loves children, Satan hates them. He is constantly, literally, and outwardly targeting your children every day.

Today many children are confused. They are sent thousands of demonic messages daily through the Internet, movies, TV, ads, music, books, social media, games, Pokémon, Harry Potter, Tarot Cards, Astrology, Eight Balls, Ouija Board, Yoga, and many more. Everything on this list is a way for Satan and his demons to enter your children's lives, unnoticed.

Satan is cunning. He places just enough "half-truths" in their lives so that your children try, but cannot understand what is real and true, and what is not. This type of thinking always brings questions to your children—who am I, who is God, and is God real? With demonic help, all of this leads to confusion, anger, disrespect, fear, condemnation, resentment, and many other evil thoughts. This confusion is meant to coerce your children's thoughts and feelings and empower them to make the wrong choices.

Demons want to deceive and draw your children away from you and God through lies and manipulation. They take what is good and twist it into what is bad. They lead your child into sin through various means—mental, emotional, and physical. They use a variety of tactics, including tempting images and exciting temptations. All of this can easily sway your child into bending to the demon's point of view. Demons are all about changing how your children see the world, how they see themselves, and how they respond to any evil influence in their lives. Instead of turning to God for their real identity, your child turns inward and listens to the demon's lies. Demons can control, discourage, deceive, oppress, and ultimately hinder children from becoming who God intends for them to be.

Deception

Paul warns Timothy about demonic false teachings that are opposed to the Gospel. Paul does not stop at simply identifying these teachings as false; he says that people who believe these false teachings about Jesus are following the "teachings of demons." This is how demons are in the service of Satan, who is the father of lies and the king of deceit. The Spirit clearly says that in later times some will abandon the faith and follow deceiving spirits and things taught by demons. Such teachings come through hypocritical liars, whose consciences have been seared as with a hot iron. They forbid people to marry and order them to abstain from certain foods, which God created to be received with thanksgiving by those who believe and who know the truth." (*1 Timothy 4:1–3*).

False Religions

The Bible seems to suggest that demonic influence actually lies behind false religions, any belief that opposes the Gospel of Jesus Christ, the Son of God. The first commandment, "You shall have no other gods before Me," (*Exodus 20:3-6*). The prohibition against making idols, bowing down to them, or serving them are definitely warnings against demonic involvement. An adult or child who questions or rejects Jesus has not just chosen a different religion. They are actually being deceived by Satan. They are unknowingly serving him and his demons. Every adult or child either believes in Jesus as the Son of God or believes some form of the teachings of demons, which are lies and deceit.

Possession

Demons can take control of your children's bodies, minds, and emotions. This is when demons exert control over your children's actions and thoughts. While the exact phrases "demonic possession or oppression" or "Deliverance" are not used, the Bible describes children being "possessed" by demons. In many accounts in the Bible, demons possess people regardless of age. Demonic possession is the total destruction of your children being possessed. For example, Jesus ordered demons to leave the body of a man who lived in the tombs. He commanded the demons to enter pigs, which then ran off a cliff and died. Only the power of Jesus could conquer and control the demons trying to steal the man's life (*Mark 5*). Demons can possess only those who have not been baptized and do not profess Jesus as their Lord and Savior. If your children have not been baptized, they are exposed to the possibility of complete demonic control over their lives.

Oppression

It is important to note that the Bible does not suggest that demons are able to possess Christians who have faith in Jesus Christ as Lord and Savior. No matter their age, if your children have been baptized and have faith in Jesus, they have the Holy Spirit living within them. Demons cannot coexist with the Holy Spirit. However, your children can still be influenced to sin and do evil through demonic attacks to their mind, body, and emotions. "Therefore take up the whole armor of God, that you may be able to withstand in the evil day, and having done all, stand firm." (*Ephesians 6:13*).

Manipulation

Demons may subtly guide your children towards destructive behaviors and choices, often appealing to their desires and vulnerabilities. This can involve tempting them with earthly possessions, pleasures, or power. They can blind unbelievers and persuade some Christians to ignore the gospel. They can empower other religions and practices that oppose Christianity. "And even if our gospel is veiled, it is veiled to those who are perishing. The god of this age has blinded the minds of unbelievers, so that they cannot see the light of the gospel that displays the glory of Christ, who is the image of God." (*2 Corinthians 4:3-4*).

Fear and Intimidation

Demons can use fear and intimidation to control and discourage children from seeking God or embracing their faith. This can involve creating a sense of powerlessness or vulnerability. "God has not given us a spirit of fear but of power, love, and of a sound mind." (*2 Timothy 1:7*). The total opposite of an intimidated spirit. So, when you are intimidated, it is a scheme of Satan and not of God.

Promoting Evil Destruction

Demons are often associated with causing harm, suffering, and chaos in the world, both physically and spiritually. The Bible describes demons as spiritual beings who actively seek to attack and influence the world through possession and temptation. These attacks take various forms, including suffering, deception, and fear. Demons' goal is to hinder God's purposes, especially concerning your children. In His sovereign plan, God allows the influence of Satan and his demons until the day of final judgment given by Jesus.

Protection from Evil

For Christian believers, no matter your age, "Put on the full armor of God, so that you can take your stand against Satan's schemes. For your struggle is not against flesh and blood, but against the rulers, against the authorities, against the powers of this dark world and against the spiritual forces of evil in the heavenly realms." (*Ephesians 6:10-12*).

Doubt and Discouragement

Demons can sow seeds of doubt and discouragement, making it harder for your children to believe in themselves or their faith. Demons may try to make them feel unworthy or hopeless. "For I am convinced that neither death nor life, neither angels nor demons, neither the present nor the future, nor any powers, neither height nor depth, nor anything else in all creation, will be able to separate us from the love of God that is in Christ Jesus our Lord." (*Romans 8:38-39*).

Pride and Self-Reliance

Demons can encourage pride and self-reliance, leading your children to believe they do not need God or His guidance. This can manifest as resistance to humility and rejection of God's authority. "A man's pride will bring him low, but a humble spirit will obtain honor." (*Proverbs 29:23).*

Division and Hatred

Demons can incite division and animosity within communities, particularly within the church. They can exploit conflicts and misunderstandings to weaken the unity of believers. As a parent, be sure to watch out and avoid those who cause divisions and create obstacles contrary to what you hold true. "I urge you, brothers and sisters, to watch out for those who cause divisions and put obstacles in your way that are contrary to the teaching you have learned." *(Romans 16:17)*.

Attacks on Faith and Hope

Demons will try to erode your children's faith and hope, making it harder for them to persevere in adversity. They may attack their sense of purpose and meaning in life. "You believe that there is one God; you do well. Even the demons believe and shudder!" (*James 2:19*).

Exploitation of Vulnerabilities

Demons often seek to exploit vulnerabilities in your children's lives, such as past hurts, unresolved issues, or unmet needs. This can involve targeting areas where your children are most susceptible to demonic influence. "For certain individuals whose condemnation was written about long ago have secretly slipped in among you. They are ungodly people, who pervert the grace of our God into a license for immorality and deny Jesus Christ our only Sovereign and Lord." (*Jude 1:4*).

Use of Temptation

Demons may use various forms of temptation to lure your children away from God, such as tempting them with material wealth, pleasures, or power. This can involve appealing to their desires and vulnerabilities. When tempted, they can say, "God is tempting me." God cannot be tempted by evil, nor does He tempt anyone. (*James 1:13-14*).

Encouragement of Idolatry

Demons may encourage idolatry by promoting the worship of false gods or the pursuit of worldly idols. This can divert your children's attention from God. "No, but the sacrifices of pagans are offered to demons, not to God, and I do not want you to be participants with demons. You cannot drink the cup of the Lord and the cup of demons too; you cannot have a part in both the Lord's table and the table of demons." *(1 Corinthians 10:20-23).*

Use of False Teachers and Teachings

Demons may use false teachers and teachings to deceive your children and lead them away from the truth. This can involve spreading misinformation, promoting false doctrines, and twisting God's Word. "In later times some will depart from the faith, giving heed to deceiving spirits and to doctrines of demons." (*1 Timothy 4:1-2*).

Demons are bent on destruction and stealing souls from God, which causes havoc for mankind. To protect your children in this spiritual war, you need to be prepared. In our society, Satan's attacks have become much bolder, more direct, and manipulative in the last fifty years. There is a spiritual war going on right now. Pray for insight and power from God the Father, Son, and Holy Spirit. Follow His lead. God loves you and your children. As you fight for your family, He will join hands with you.

CHAPTER 5

The Bible and Spiritual Warfare

There are two primary errors when it comes to spiritual warfare: over-emphasis and under-emphasis. Some blame every sin, every conflict, and every problem on demons that need to be cast out. Others completely ignore the spiritual realm and the fact that the Bible describes our battle as against spiritual powers. The key to successful spiritual warfare is finding the biblical balance. Jesus sometimes cast demons out of people; other times, He healed people with no mention of the demonic.

The Apostle Paul Instructs You to Wage War Against The Sin In Yourself

"What shall we say, then? Shall we go on sinning so that grace may increase? By no means! We are those who have died to sin; how can we live in it any longer? Or don't you know that all of us who were baptized into Christ Jesus were baptized into his death? We were therefore buried with him through baptism into death in order that, just as Christ was raised from the dead through the glory of the Father, we too may live a new life.

For if we have been united with him in a death like his, we will certainly also be united with him in a resurrection like his. For we know that our old self was crucified with him so that the body ruled by sin might be done away with, that we should no longer be slaves to sin, because anyone who has died has been set free from sin.

Now if we died with Christ, we believe that we will also live with him. For we know that since Christ was raised from the dead, he cannot die again; death no longer has mastery over him. The death he died, he died to sin once for all; but the life he lives, he lives to God.

In the same way, count yourselves dead to sin but alive to God in Christ Jesus. Therefore, do not let sin reign in your mortal body so that you obey its evil desires. Do not offer any part of yourself to sin as an instrument of wickedness, but rather offer yourselves to God as those who have been brought from death to life, and offer every part of yourself to him as an instrument of righteousness. For sin shall no longer be your master, because you are not under the law, but under grace.

What then? Shall we sin because we are not under the law but under grace? By no means! Don't you know that when you offer yourselves to someone as obedient slaves, you are slaves of the one you obey—whether you are slaves to sin, which leads to death, or to obedience, which leads to righteousness? But thanks be to God that, though you used to be slaves to sin, you have come to obey from your heart the pattern of teaching that has now claimed your allegiance. You have been set free from sin and have become slaves to righteousness. I am using an example from everyday life because of your human limitations. Just as you used to offer yourselves as slaves to impurity and to ever-increasing wickedness, so now offer yourselves as slaves to righteousness leading to holiness. When you were slaves to sin, you were free from the control of righteousness. What benefit did you reap at that time from the things you are now ashamed of? Those things result in death! But now that you have been set free from sin and have become slaves of God, the benefit you reap leads to holiness, and the result is eternal life. For the wages of sin is death, but the gift of God is eternal life in[b] Christ Jesus our Lord." *(Romans 6:1-23)*.

The Bible Also Warns You to Oppose The Schemes of Satan

"Finally, be strong in the Lord and in his mighty power. Put on the full armor of God, so that you can take your stand against the devil's schemes. For our struggle is not against flesh and blood but against the rulers, against the authorities, against the powers of this dark world and against the spiritual forces of evil in the heavenly realms."

This describes the spiritual armor God gives you.

"Put on the full armor of God, so that you can take your stand against the devil's schemes. For our struggle is not against flesh and blood, but against the rulers, against the authorities, against the powers of this dark world and against the spiritual forces of evil in the heavenly realms. ¹Therefore put on the full armor of God, so that when the day of evil comes, you may be able to stand your ground, and after you have done everything, to stand. Stand firm then, with the belt of truth buckled around your waist, with the breastplate of righteousness in place, and with your feet fitted with the readiness that comes from the gospel of peace. In addition to all this, take up the shield of faith, with which you can extinguish all the flaming arrows of the evil one. Take the helmet of salvation and the sword of the Spirit, which is the word of God." *(Ephesians 6:10-18)*.

When Entering Spiritual Warfare, Realize

- Spiritual Armor is to be used in spiritual warfare.
- Know God's truth, believe God's truth, and speak God's truth.
- You are to declare and live a righteous life because of Christ's sacrifice for you.
- Proclaim the Gospel and its truth.
- Do not waver in your faith; trust the promises God made to you.

Your ultimate defense is your salvation, and no demonic power can steal that from you. In spiritual warfare, the primary offensive weapon is the Word of God, as revealed in the Bible. Prayer is the power and will of the Holy Spirit.

Jesus is your ultimate example of resisting temptation. Look at how Jesus handled direct attacks from Satan when He was tempted in the wilderness. "Then Jesus was led by the Spirit into the wilderness to be tempted by the devil. After fasting forty days and forty nights, he was hungry. Satan came to Him and said, 'If you are the Son of God, tell these stones to become bread.' Jesus answered, 'It is written: "Man shall not live on bread alone, but on every word that comes from the mouth of God." Then the devil took Him to the holy city and had Him stand on the highest point of the temple. 'If you are the Son of God,' He said, 'throw yourself down. For it is written: "He will command His angels concerning you, and they will lift you up in their hands, so that you will not strike your foot against a stone."' Jesus answered him, 'It is also written: "Do not put the Lord your God to the test."' Again, the devil took Him to a very high mountain and showed Him all the kingdoms of the world and their splendor. 'All this I will give you,' he said, 'if you will bow down and worship me.' Jesus said to him, 'Away from me, Satan! For it is written: "Worship the Lord your God, and serve Him only."' Then the devil left Him, and angels came and attended Him." *(Matthew 4:1–11)*.

The Bible is the most powerful weapon against the temptations of the devil: "I have hidden your word in my heart that I might not sin against you." *(Psalm 119:11)*.

A word of caution concerning spiritual warfare: you are only human. All authority comes from God. Here is an example of what can happen when people presume an authority they have not been given: "Some Jews who went around driving out evil spirits tried to invoke the name of the Lord Jesus over those who were demon-possessed. They would say, 'In the name of Jesus whom Paul preaches, I command you to come out.' Seven sons of Sceva, a Jewish chief priest, were doing this. One day the evil spirit answered them, 'Jesus I know, and Paul I know about, but who are you?' Then the man who had the evil spirit jumped on them and overpowered them all.

He gave them such a beating that they ran out of the house naked and bleeding." *(Acts 19:13-16).*

Without belief and faith in the Lord Jesus Christ, believing He is the Son of God, and through Jesus, the authority to cast out demons is given, the seven sons had no power against the demons they were trying to cast out. All power and authority to cast out demons comes from God.

Pray directly to God the Father, God the Son, and God the Holy Spirit every day. It is through God that all your protection comes.

Do not have a conversation directly with the demon; you run the risk of being led astray, as Eve was. You are mortal and need the power of our Lord Jesus Christ to deal directly with all demons.

"Now the serpent was craftier than any of the wild animals the Lord God had made. He said to the woman, 'Did God really say, "You must not eat from any tree in the garden?"' The woman said to the serpent, 'We may eat fruit from the trees in the garden, but God did say, "You must not eat fruit from the tree that is in the middle of the garden, and you must not touch it, or you will die."' 'You will not certainly die,' the serpent said to the woman. 'For God knows that when you eat from it your eyes will be opened, and you will be like God, knowing good and evil.' When the woman saw that the fruit of the tree was good for food and pleasing to the eye, and also desirable for gaining wisdom, she took some and ate it. She also gave some to her husband, who was with her, and he ate it. Then the eyes of both of them were opened, and they realized they were naked; so they sewed fig leaves together and made coverings for themselves." *(Genesis 3:1–7).*

Submit yourself to God's will. Keep your focus on God, not demons. You are loved by God, protected by the Holy Spirit, and through the power of the Lord Jesus Christ, you are given the ability to perform His will in the world.

The Keys To Success In Spiritual Warfare

- Rely on God's power, not your own.

- Put on the whole Armor of God. Draw on the power of the Bible—the Word of God is the Holy Spirit's sword. The Sword of the Spirit, the Word of God, is used to defend against attacking demons. Never take off your armor. Check your spiritual well-being each day to ensure your armor is securely fastened.

- Stand firm with others. "Therefore put on the full armor of God, so that when the day of evil comes, you may be able to stand your ground, and after you have done everything, to stand. Stand firm then, with the belt of truth buckled around your waist, with the breastplate of righteousness in place." *(Ephesians 6:13–14)*.

- Submit your prayers to Jesus. Never appeal directly to demons or Satan, only through Jesus. He has all power and authority, so we always say "In the name of Jesus Christ".

- Submit to God and resist Satan's schemes: "Submit yourselves, then, to God. Resist the devil, and he will flee from you, knowing that the Lord of hosts is your protector." *(James 4:7)*.

- "Truly he is my rock and my salvation; he is my fortress, I will never be shaken." *(Psalm 62:2)*.

Spiritual Warfare

Within Christianity, spiritual warfare is a concept that involves a battle against demons. It recognizes the unseen conflict. As a parent, you need wisdom and discernment to know what is natural and what is not. You also need to understand how and when spiritual warfare affects your children. Through faith, prayer, and obedience to God, you can actively resist the influence of demons in your children's lives

Spiritual Warfare Is

- Recognizing the reality of spiritual conflict.
- Understanding the demonic tactics and strategies.
- Reaching out to God for power and guidance.
- Living in obedience and faith.
- Relying on God's promises for victory.

The Reality of Spiritual Warfare

It Is Not Just A Concept

Spiritual warfare is about acknowledging the reality of evil spiritual forces and their potential to negatively impact your or your child's life.

Demonic Activity Is Real

Scriptures, such as the Gospels, show instances where Jesus encountered and cast out demons, demonstrating their power and influence.

It Is Not Always Dramatic

While some battles might involve dramatic displays, spiritual warfare can also appear subtly—in your mind, emotions, and body.

Deception Is The Primary Weapon

Demons associated with Satan use deception to mislead and confuse you.

Spiritual Darkness

Demons seek to create darkness, hinder, and separate you from your relationship with God.

Personal Attacks

Demons can target you with lies and temptations.

Jesus Has Authority

Jesus has authority over the spirit world, and Christians can draw on that authority.

The Power Of God's Word

God's Word, the Bible, is a powerful weapon against demons.

Prayer Is Essential

Prayer connects you to God's power and is your way to ask for protection and guidance.

Armor Of God

Spiritual armor acts as your shield of faith. Each piece protects you from demonic attacks. The Sword of Righteousness, the Word, is an offensive weapon.

Seek God's Wisdom

Ask God to reveal His will and guide your actions during spiritual attacks.

Living In Obedience

Being obedient to God involves worship, prayer, rest, and reflection, which helps you get closer to Him.

Morality

God requires you not to commit murder, adultery, theft, coveting, lying, and more. A moral life strengthens your spiritual armor and helps you resist the enemy.

Desires

Do not be envious or desire what belongs to others or anything that serves demons and not God.

Truth Is the Ultimate Weapon

Standing firm in the truth of The Bible, God's Word, is a powerful way to overcome demonic lies.

Repentance and Confession

When you sin or make a mistake, confess it to God, repent, and accept His forgiveness and love.

Do Not Despair

Even during spiritual attacks, remain hopeful in God's promises and trust His power and love.

Key Passages About Spiritual Warfare

This passage offers a comprehensive teaching on spiritual warfare, urging you to "put on the full armor of God" and to resist Satan's schemes. It reminds that your battle is not against flesh and blood but against "the rulers, the authorities, the cosmic powers over this present darkness, and the spiritual forces of evil in the heavenly places." *(Ephesians 6:10-18)*.

Another passage highlights your weapons in spiritual warfare, which are not physical but "mighty before God" as you demolish strongholds and take captive every thought. It commands you to resist arguments and pretenses set against the knowledge of God. *(2 Corinthians 10:4-5)*.

This verse describes cosmic battles between Michael and his angels against the dragon and his fallen angels. *(Revelation 12:7)*.

You can be assured you are "more than conquerors" in all struggles. *(Romans 8:3)*.

You are to remain alert and sober-minded against temptation by Satan. *(1 Peter 5:8-9)*.

You are promised no weapon formed against believers will prosper and that you will refute every accusing tongue. *(Isaiah 54:17)*.

Parents Must Be Alert and Trained

Demons affect individuals, including children, in various ways. Signs of demonic attack include behavioral changes, unusual occurrences, and physical and mental illness. Intense anxiety or depression in children can also be manifestations of demonic attacks.

In some cases, physical illnesses may be linked to demonic attacks, but not all illnesses are demonic. You need to understand that attributing all illness to demons can harm your child. Always seek advice from medical doctors and psychologists. Do not hinder access to necessary medical or psychological care if it is needed.

Demons twist the truth and can convince your child that their lies are true. It is essential to speak truth into their lies, but you must first know what is true. We live in a world where truth is often rejected and replaced with opinions, especially about religion and morality. This is why some Christian children and parents can be fooled. Many today see the Christian faith as a personal preference instead of the explanation of all reality.

As a parent, you must be alert and trained to protect your children. Society often lacks a moral compass. People readily tell you what to believe with no room for error. Many struggle to discuss their own spiritual life. "What's true for you is true for you, and what's true for me is true for me," is a common belief. Some people insist, "I am right, so you must be wrong."

Today, many consider religion and morality to be ignorant or stupid. With such beliefs widespread in adults, it is no wonder children are confused. Truth is being in accordance with fact or reality, the opposite of falsehood. It describes a statement or belief that aligns with how things really are. Truth is a proven concept accepted in many fields of thought. Teaching your children about how truth works lays a foundation for their clear thinking about spiritual beliefs. Truth always lines up with what is real. But society operates differently, defining truth subjectively. Today, it is something we create within ourselves for ourselves. Truth is what I think, and what I think is the absolute truth.

What you believe about God and right and wrong is extremely important. From an early age, teach your child the truth about Christian spirituality and morality. "And if Christ has not been raised, then our preaching is in vain, and your faith is in vain." *(1 Corinthians 15:14)* Jesus' resurrection either happened or it did not. As a Christian, it did. Your salvation is based on Jesus' death, burial, and resurrection. It is your responsibility to share this truth with your children.

Equip your children with knowledge of God's truth. Knowing God's truth helps them resist demonic lies and deception. Satan, the father of lies, uses many modern avenues—social media, movies, cartoons, video games, music, television, books, educational resources, and more—to reach your children. Their welfare is at stake. It is time for you to enter the fight. Your weapons are not physical but spiritual: obedience and faith in God, the Armor of God, prayer, and partnering with Jesus to free children and adults. These gifts enable you to overcome demonic activity. "For though we live in the world, we do not wage war as the world does. The weapons we fight with are not the weapons of the world. On the contrary, they have divine power to cast out demons. We demolish arguments and every pretension that sets itself up against the knowledge of God, and we take captive every thought to make it obedient to Christ. And we will be ready to punish every act of disobedience, once your obedience is complete." *(2 Corinthians 10:3-6).*

Direct Disobedience by Your Child

When your child disobeys God, this disobedience can open the door for demons to come into their lives. Sometimes your children do not realize they have done anything wrong. This can make everything in their lives suddenly irrational. When you sense unease, ask God to help you identify the causes of the bad behavior.

Pray for Wisdom and Guidance

"Father, help me to respond to my child's disobedience in ways that honor Your love and wisdom. Give me patience and understanding, and help me remember that I am parenting with You."

Pray for a Change of Heart

"Lord, open my child's eyes to see their disobedience as sin, not just a mistake. Help them understand the importance of honoring You and obeying Your commands. Draw them to You and help them find joy in their relationship with Christ."

Pray for God's Grace and Self-Control

"Father, help me respond to my child's disobedience with grace and self-control, even when it is difficult. Fill me with Your Spirit so I can correct lovingly and graciously."

Pray for Understanding and Mercy

"Lord, help me understand the reasons for my child's disobedience—whether it is due to a lack of understanding, fear, or something else. Grant me mercy and compassion, and help me see my child through Your eyes."

Pray for God's Love and Purpose

"Father, I know You love my children unconditionally, even when they disobey. Help me remember You have a purpose for their lives and are guiding them, even in difficult times. Help me trust Your plan and parent faithfully according to Your Word."

"And, fathers, do not provoke your children to anger, but bring them up in the training and discipline of the Lord." *(Ephesians 6:4).*

"He who disciplines his child will give him rest, and he will make his heart happy." *(Proverbs 29:17).*

Spiritual Warfare Weapons God Gave Parents

Conversations with Your Children

Satan is trying to indoctrinate your children. As your children grow closer to Jesus, God calls you to provide a healthy spiritual environment for them. There are many ways to do this. For example, at supper, share about their day, pray with them daily, ask if they need help, read and discuss the Bible together, and take time for conversations. Be creative about how you and your child can spend time with God. "Start children off on the way they should go, and even when they are old they will not turn from it." *(Proverbs 22:6).*

It is very important to start early, having frequent conversations with your children about modern-day culture. For example, today we face a dominant worldview indoctrinating children into acceptance of radical gender theory, presenting it as good and true. This undermines God's design for two distinct genders, marriage, and procreation. Christian parents can introduce their children to God's design as early as age three or four and continue the discussion through their teen years.

Talk to your children and answer their questions about God and His will. Any conversation done in love is good. If your child asks a difficult question you do not have the answer for, say, "Why don't we look it up and find the answer together?" You do not have to be a Bible scholar to handle tough questions. Taking time to find answers together can be fun and helpful.

"God blessed them and said to them, 'Be fruitful and increase in number; fill the earth and subdue it. Rule over the fish in the sea and the birds in the sky and over every living creature that moves on the ground." *(Genesis 1:28).*

"When God created man, he made him in the likeness of God. Male and female he created them, and he blessed them." *(Genesis 5:1-2).*

Pray for Your Children

Prayer is a mighty weapon against Satan. God wants you to be consistent in praying, listening, and teaching. "You shall teach them diligently to your children, and shall talk of them when you sit in your house, and when you walk by the way, and when you lie down, and when you rise." *(Deuteronomy 6:7).*

Prepare yourself with knowledge. In faith, guide your children, talk with them, and pray for their protection and growth. There is great power in prayer. Pray daily with thanksgiving for your children. Release all fears and concerns to God. Ask Him to bless and watch over your children. Ask Him to guide you and your children walkthrough life. Pray for protection over their days and nights. Pray blessings over them, no matter what happened during the day.

God promises to fill your heart and mind with His immeasurable peace. "Do not be anxious about anything, but in every situation, by prayer and petition, with thanksgiving, present your requests to God. And the peace of God, which transcends all understanding, will guard your hearts and your minds in Christ Jesus." *(Philippians 4:6-7).*

Fight for your children. Speak truth into the lies. Even in this chaotic culture, train your children to stand strong in Jesus.

There are many prayers available as you pray with and for your children. Of course, a prayer from your heart is always the best.

Dear God,

I ask for help me to remember to always keep Your Armor on every day. You give me all I need to stand firm in this world. Forgive me, God, for the times I have been unprepared, too busy to care, or tried to fight evil with my own strength. Thank You that I never fight alone, for You are constantly at work on my behalf—shielding, protecting, strengthening, exposing deeds of darkness, and bringing to light what needs to be known. Even when I am unaware, You cover me from the cruel attacks I face daily. Thank You, dear Lord, for Your love, protection, and guidance. Amen

Dear God,

Today I put on the full Armor of God to guard my life against attack. I put on the Belt of Truth to protect against lies and deception. I put on the Breastplate of Righteousness to protect my heart from temptations I battle. I put the Gospel of Peace on my feet, so we are ready to take Your light, wherever You find me. I choose to walk in the peace and freedom of Your Spirit and not be overcome by fear and anxious thoughts.

I take up Your Shield of Faith, which will extinguish all darts and threats hurled our way by the enemy. I believe in Your power to protect me and my family. I choose to trust in You. I put on the Helmet of Salvation, which covers my mind and thoughts, reminding me I am a child of God— forgiven, set free, and saved by the grace of Christ Jesus. I take up the Sword of the Spirit, Your very Word, the one offensive weapon You gave me for battle, which has the power to demolish strongholds, alive and active, and sharper than any two-edged sword. Amen

The Armor of God

The Armor of God is given to you and your children to resist Satan. It is a metaphor for the spiritual protection and strength available to Christians in their battle with evil. It is a call to equip yourself with God's resources and stand firm against the "schemes of Satan."

James 1:21: "Therefore, put away all filthiness and rampant wickedness and receive with meekness the implanted word, which is able to save your souls."

James 4:7: "Submit yourselves therefore to God. Resist the devil, and he will flee from you."

How To Put on The Armor of God

You "put on" the Armor of God through prayer and intentional focus on the spiritual principles below. This means consciously aligning your thoughts, attitudes, and actions with these truths daily and relying on God's strength to help you live by them. Regular prayer, Bible study, and fellowship with other believers are vital. Never take off your armor.

- Finding God by reading scripture and through prayer keeps your mind on God, not worldly things.
- Trust God knows what is best for you and your children.
- Be thankful for God's love, care, and what it means for you and your family.

The Armor of God

"Finally, be strong in the Lord and in his mighty power. Put on the full armor of God, so that you can take your stand against the devil's schemes. For our struggle is not against flesh and blood, but against the rulers, the authorities, against the powers of this dark world and against the spiritual forces of evil in the heavenly realms. Therefore, put on the full armor of God, so that when the day of evil comes, you may be able to stand your ground, and after you have done everything, to stand. Stand firm then." *(Ephesians 6:10-17).*

The Belt of Truth

Fasten the belt by standing in God's truth. Identify lies you may believe.

"Therefore, my beloved brethren whom I long to see, my joy and crown, in this way stand firm in the Lord, my beloved." *(Philippians 4:1).*

"See to it that no one takes you captive by philosophy and empty deceit, according to human tradition, according to the elemental spirits of the world, and not according to Christ." *(Colossians 2:8).*

"For the weapons of our warfare are not of the flesh but have divine power to destroy strongholds. We destroy arguments and every lofty opinion raised against the knowledge of God and take every thought captive to obey Christ." *(2 Corinthians 10:4-5).*

"I have been crucified with Christ. It is no longer I who live, but Christ who lives in me. And the life I now live in the flesh I live by faith in the Son of God, who loved me and gave himself for me." *(Galatians 2:20).*

The Sword of The Spirit

As an offensive and defensive weapon from the Holy Spirit, all Christian soldiers need ongoing training to use the Sword of the Spirit—the Word of God. (*2 Timothy 3:16-17).*

"All Scripture is God-breathed and is useful for teaching, rebuking, correcting and training in righteousness, so that the servant of God may be thoroughly equipped for every good work." *(2 Timothy 3:16).*

"For the weapons of our warfare are not of the flesh but have divine power to destroy strongholds. We destroy arguments and every lofty opinion raised against the knowledge of God and take every thought captive to obey Christ." *(2 Corinthians 10:4-5)*.

"For the word of God is living and active, sharper than any two-edged sword, piercing to the division of soul and spirit, of joints and marrow, and discerning the thoughts and intentions of the heart." *(Hebrews 4:12)*.

"Teach me, Lord, the way of your decrees, that I may follow it to the end. Give me understanding, so that I may keep your law and obey it with all my heart. Direct me in the path of your commands, for there I find delight. Turn my heart toward your statutes and not toward selfish gain. Turn my eyes away from worthless things; preserve my life according to your word. Fulfill your promise to your servant so that you may be feared. Take away the disgrace I dread, for your laws are good. How I long for your precepts! In your righteousness preserve my life." *(Psalm 119:33-40)*.

Breastplate Of Righteousness

The Breastplate represents the protection given by righteousness, shielding your heart, mind, and soul from the fiery darts of the evil one. *(Ephesians 6:14)*.

"Be found in him, not having a righteousness of my own that comes from the law, but that which is through faith in Christ—the righteousness that comes from God on the basis of faith." *(Philippians 3:9)*.

"But if we walk in the light, as he is in the light, we have fellowship with one another, and the blood of Jesus his Son cleanses us from all sin." *(1 John 1:7)*.

"If we confess our sins, he is faithful and just and will forgive us our sins and purify us from all unrighteousness." *(1 John 1:9)*.

Shoes Of Peace

Provides readiness and preparation to share the good news of Jesus. Standing firm in faith is essential *(Ephesians 6:15)*.

"This peace rules in your hearts, to which you were also called in one body; and be thankful." *(Colossians 3:15)*.

"What you have learned and received and heard and seen in me—practice these things, and the God of Peace will be with you." *(Philippians 4:9)*.

Shield Of Faith

Protects you from spiritual attacks, extinguishing all flaming arrows of the evil one, throwing the enemy off guard.

"Be alert and of sober mind. Your enemy the devil prowls around like a roaring lion looking for someone to devour. ^{9} Resist him, standing firm in the faith, because you know that the family of believers throughout the world is undergoing the same kind of sufferings." *(1 Peter 5:8-9)*.

"For by grace you have been saved through faith. And this is not your own doing; it is the gift of God." *(Ephesians 2:8)*.

"And whatever you ask in prayer, you will receive if you have faith." *(Matthew 21:22)*.

"Is anyone among you sick? Let them call the elders of the church to pray over them and anoint them with oil in the name of the Lord. ^{15} And the prayer offered in faith will make the sick person well; the Lord will raise them up. If they have sinned, they will be forgiven." *(James 5:14-15)*.

Helmet Of Salvation

Represents the hope and assurance of salvation from God, It protects your mind against the darkness of this world. It signifies your secure identity and protection in Christ, ensuring you are on God's side in spiritual battles.

"The Lord looked and was displeased that there was no justice. He saw that there was no one; he was appalled that there was no one to intervene, so his own arm achieved salvation for him, and his own righteousness sustained him. He put on righteousness as his breastplate, and the helmet of salvation on his head; he put on garments of vengeance and wrapped himself in zeal as in a cloak." *(Isaiah 59:16-17).*

"But since we belong to the day, let us be sober, putting on faith and love as a breastplate, and the hope of salvation as a helmet." *(1 Thessalonians 5:8).*

Check your Armor of God daily through prayer and meditation to make sure your armor is securely on and ready for battle. It is a gift from God to protect and defend you and your family from harm.

Never take your armor off.

Be prepared at all times.

Read, Pray, and Memorize Scripture

Parents Do Spiritual Warfare

As a parent, you help protect your children by actively engaging in spiritual warfare. There are ways to guard your family: prayer, teaching the truth of God's Word, attending church, being a positive example, rejecting demonic lies and temptations, and living as God wants you to live. You may not always understand why hard times happen, but your response is the same: faith, prayer, Scripture, and perseverance.

Understanding How Satan Works

You need to recognize when a spiritual battle is ongoing and the enemy is actively trying to deceive and destroy you and your children. Satan often leads us into sin through temptation, deception, and accusations. Teach your children to recognize these tactics in an age-appropriate way. The goal is to prepare them, not scare them.

Seeking God's Guidance and Protection

God offers you His guidance through prayer, the Bible, and your personal experiences. This guidance requires recognizing and following God's direction in your everyday decisions, big and small.

As a parent seeking God's guidance and protection for your family, you are building a personal relationship with Him. It is characterized by trust, faith, and a willingness to follow His direction. This relationship is developed through prayer, studying the Bible, and seeking counsel from others. Prepare yourself and your family by asking God to cover all of you in His armor. This armor will help you and your family as you stand firm against demonic attacks. Also, pray for your own and for your children's safety.

Your success in spiritual warfare rests on building a close relationship with God, continuously resisting Satan and his demons, and building a strong spiritual foundation for your family.

Be Intentional

Your decisions have consequences for you and your family. The people around you impact you and your children positively or negatively. Your family's circle of friends matters—they influence you and your children.

Satan can access your children through their friends. The wrong friend can lead them astray. He can use friends or neighbors to plant doubt. Remember, your enemy is not the people you or your children are around, but the demons influencing them. These people may be under demonic influence. As a Christian, you are called to pray for them. As a parent, guard your family from all evil by praying for protection in Jesus' name.

Be On Guard

Peace can be shattered suddenly. When trouble comes, it can feel overwhelming. Know that trouble is bound to happen, so be prepared for it.

"Dear friends, do not be surprised at the fiery ordeal that has come on you to test you, as though something strange were happening to you." *(1 Peter 4:12).*

This truth helps you prepare mentally and spiritually. You will face challenges in this life. While this might not be great news, knowing this can help you shift your mindset and prepare you for what is to come.

If Jesus was persecuted, you can expect the same. "If they persecuted me, they will persecute you also." *(John 15:20).*

"Be alert and of sober mind. Your enemy the devil prowls around like a roaring lion looking for someone to devour. Resist him, standing firm in the faith, because you know that the family of believers throughout the world is undergoing the same kind of sufferings." *(1 Peter 5:8).*

You know challenges will come. Your first strategy is to be vigilant and ready. Be assured, your family will face resistance.

Remember Who the Battle Is With

Just as Satan tried to tempt Jesus in the wilderness, he will tempt you and your children. Stay alert, aware, and pray against negative influences affecting your family. Sometimes bad things happen without a clear reason. These moments teach perseverance, strength, and resilience. The key is faith in God's compassion, love, and understanding. He will give you the strength to rise again and continue the fight.

"Finally, be strong in the Lord and in his mighty power. Put on the full armor of God so that you can take your stand against the devil's schemes. For our struggle is not against flesh and blood, but against the rulers, authorities, powers of this dark world, and spiritual forces of evil in the heavenly realms." *(Ephesians 6:10-12).*

It is easy to forget the real battle is not with people but spiritual forces. You cannot defeat these forces on your own. You need God's help; He has already defeated Satan. God has power and control over all, including Satan.

You can only stand firm through the Lord's power. God's armor protects you, and your battle is against spiritual forces. "Finally, be strong in the Lord and in his mighty power." *(Ephesians 6:10).*

"The weapons we fight with are not the weapons of the world. On the contrary, they have divine power to demolish strongholds. We demolish arguments and every pretension that sets itself up against the knowledge of God, and we take captive every thought to make it obedient to Christ." *(2 Corinthians 10:4-5).*

God does not expect you to defeat Satan alone. He equips you with tools for the battle. Your primary defense is God. So, know Him better, read His Word, understand His promises, and depend on Him in prayer.

Read the Bible

Memorize Scriptures so that you can call on them in times of trouble. The Holy Spirit will bring them to mind when needed. This will help you and your children through all challenges. Better yet, memorize passages as a family.

Knowing and meditating on Scripture equips you to stand strong in spiritual battles. It helps you discern true thoughts from enemy attacks. Remember, you cannot fight spiritual battles alone or with worldly weapons.

God does not act like Satan who speaks lies. God does not throw darts of doubt, guilt, or shame. Negative thoughts always come from Satan. Remember God's promise to always be your helper and never forsake you. *(Hebrews 13:5-6)*.

Prayer

Few things in your life can actually be controlled; prayer is one of them. It is a way to ask for God's protection and guidance over your family. You can present your requests to Him, trusting He knows what is best for you. Prayer is a request, not a demand. God loves you and will never betray you. Prayer is crucial to defeating Satan. Because of Jesus' great love, He empowers you to overcome Satan and his demons.

Your children may not understand the threats of demons or prayer's power. You are called to pray for and with them. Jesus modeled prayer in every situation. He told Peter, James, and John to pray so they would not fall into temptation. Jesus often prayed alone, listening to God, and meditating on His message. "Watch and pray so that you will not fall into temptation. The spirit is willing, but the flesh is weak." *(Matthew 26:41)*.

Jesus taught the Lord's Prayer and how you should pray: "But when you pray, go into your room, close the door and pray to your Father, who is unseen. Then your Father, who sees what is done in secret, will reward you." *(Matthew 6:6).*

Pray daily for yourself, your children, and your family's spiritual well-being, pray against demonic attacks, asking for protection, and seeking wisdom and discernment.

Teaching God's Truth

You have the responsibility to teach your children about God's truth as it is shown in the Bible, explaining God's love, grace, and truth, and exposing Satan's lies and deception.

Christianity teaches "God is Truth," meaning God's knowledge and wisdom are perfect, and anything not in line with Him is false. God is trustworthy, always truthful, and consistent. His Word is always a reliable source of guidance and truth.

Be an Example

You must live out your faith daily, maintaining a strong relationship with God and commitment to His teachings. Practice humility, forgiveness, obedience, and exhibit the fruit of the Spirit—love, joy, peace, patience, kindness, goodness, faithfulness, gentleness, and self-control.

Attend Church

Church offers opportunities to learn about God, deepen your Bible knowledge, and grow in faith. It benefits your family spiritually and socially, providing community and support. It is a place to worship, learn God's Word, connect with believers, and receive encouragement.

Attend church regularly with your children. Discuss their church experiences. Ask what they learned and how it affects their relationship with God, Jesus, and the Holy Spirit.

Rejecting Lies and Temptations

Rejecting lies and temptations is vital to living a righteous and God honoring life. It involves actively fighting deceitful thoughts and urges leading to sin. Reject sinful behaviors, refuse harmful influences, and speak truth against lies. Pray against the demon's lies and temptations targeting your children.

- Ground yourself in the truth found in the Bible.
- Recognize and address your weakness
- Realize you have a choice
- Resist temptation immediately
- Lean on God and pray for strength
- Practice honesty and acceptance
- Consider the consequences
- Avoid justifying dishonesty

CHAPTER 6
Demonic Footholds

Spiritual footholds are situations, circumstances, or behavior patterns that provide opportunities for demonic influence to enter your life. "Demonic footholds" are secure, strategic positions from which demons can advance. These footholds represent areas where Satan can enter and exert his influence. He can gain access through your various actions and attitudes, creating opportunities to pull you into despair and doubt. The psalmist cried out to God, "I sink in the murky depths, where there is no foothold. I have come into the deep waters; the floods engulf me." *(Psalm 69:2)*.

Satan seeks to establish a strategic position in your life. It may start simply—holding on to anger, grudges, bitterness, and so forth. Once Satan establishes a foothold, he continually finds ways to advance in your life, spreading lies and temptations. If you give Satan a foothold in your life, he will find it easier to attack you and separate you from God. Spiritual footholds will build up into spiritual strongholds through habitual thought patterns or mental fortresses that hinder your faith and obedience to God. "And do not give the devil a foothold." *(Ephesians 4:27)*.

Addressing satanic footholds is part of spiritual warfare. It involves resisting evil and seeking God's protection. Understanding footholds and choosing to prevent or remove them frees you from being influenced by demons. Paul exhorts dealing with negative emotions quickly: "Do not let the sun go down while you are still angry, for anger gives a foothold to the devil." *(Ephesians 4:26b-27)*.

Giving Demons A Foothold

Certain negative behaviors, thoughts, attitudes, or sins can give demons opportunities to gain footholds in your life. Unresolved issues or persistent sins create vulnerabilities that allow demons to influence your mind, body, and emotions.

Footholds Entry Points

Foothold entry points include unforgiveness, anger, resentment, bitterness, gossip, lust, pride, persistent sin, and lack of faith in God. Negative emotions and behaviors provide demons with points of entry. Patterns of behavior or circumstances become opportunities for demonic influence.

The Impact of Footholds

Allowing footholds to take root will open yourself up to further spiritual harm. Once established, demons make situations worse, which leads to more severe problems like mental and emotional distress, addictions, or physical ailments.

Breaking Footholds

Recognizing footholds and addressing them through prayer, repentance, confession, and seeking God's guidance can break demonic footholds and reclaim your spiritual freedom.

Generational Footholds

Negative behaviors or sins can be passed down through generations, creating generational footholds that need to be addressed. "The Lord will by no means clear the guilty but will visit the iniquity of the fathers on the children and grandchildren to the third and fourth generation." *(Exodus 34:7).*

At conversion, Christians enter a spiritual army involved in Spiritual Warfare, You become an enemy of Satan. *(Ephesians 6:10-12).*

Paul warns you not to give the devil a foothold: "Do not let the sun go down while you are still angry, and do not give the devil a foothold." *(Ephesians 4:26-27).*

Demonic Strongholds

The word strongholds appears once in the New Testament and is used symbolically by Paul to describe Christian spiritual warfare.

"For though we live in the world, we do not wage war as the world does. The weapons we fight with are not the weapons of the world. On the contrary, they have divine power to demolish strongholds. We demolish arguments and every pretension that sets itself up against the knowledge of God, and we take captive every thought to make it obedient to Christ. Though we walk in the flesh, we do not war according to the flesh, for the weapons of our warfare are not of the flesh, but divinely powerful for the destruction of fortresses [strongholds]." *(2 Corinthians 10:3-5)*.

Spiritual Strongholds are habitual thought patterns or mental fortresses in which demons gather. This can prevent you from growing in faith and living according to God's will. They are often rooted in lies or negative beliefs that have become deeply ingrained, making it hard to break free from them. They manifest in ways such as limiting perceptions, negative emotions, dysfunctional behaviors, or resistance to change. Demonic strongholds are like fortified areas of demons that affect a Christian's mind, emotions, and body. Non-believers' strongholds include the mind, emotions, body, and soul.

All strongholds resist God's truth and hinder spiritual growth. Recognizing and breaking these strongholds through truth, prayer, and spiritual warfare is essential for experiencing true freedom and an abundant life. Strongholds are not demons themselves, but demonic forces can work within them by developing demonic interferences, such as negative or evil habitual thinking and behaviors. Demons create barriers to you doing God's work in the world. Demons can keep you from thinking clearly, accepting the truth, stopping sin, and receiving Deliverance.

Strongholds support confusion, fear, anger, unforgiveness, etc. They develop with repeated exposure to negative thoughts, unbiblical beliefs, harmful behavior, childhood trauma, societal pressures, and personal choices; as well as disobeying God's Word, ignoring His counsel, and self-worship.

Recognizing strongholds means identifying recurring negative thoughts or behavior patterns that are hard or seem impossible to change. The demons within the Stronghold always oppose God's truth.

Breaking Spiritual Strongholds

To overcome strongholds, you must commit to identifying and dismantling negative patterns in your thinking and behavior. This process involves prayer, repentance, confessing sins, seeking God's guidance, and perhaps Deliverance.

Breaking strongholds means repenting of sin and generational curses, replacing lies with truth, false beliefs with God's truth, and harmful habits with healthy choices.

Open Doors

How Demons Gain Access to Your Life

God sees the human body as a dwelling place. Scripture calls the body of the believer the temple of the Holy Spirit. *(1 Corinthians 6:19).* But Satan and his demons also see the human body as a place to live. *(Matthew 12:43-45).*

"When an unclean spirit goes out of a man, he goes through dry places, seeking rest, and finds none. Then he says, 'I will return to my house from which I came.' And when he comes, he finds it empty, swept, and put in order. Then he goes and takes with him seven other spirits more wicked than himself, and they enter and dwell there; and the last state of that man is worse than the first."

The demon in this passage refers to the man as his house. Demons crave bodies to live in and to express their nature through. A demon cannot simply enter into any person that they choose; there must be an open door in the house for it to have entrance. Several things can open the door for demonic access into your life. These open doors give demons a place to enter and dwell in the person.

Descriptions Of Some Open Doors

Ongoing Sin

When you fail to confess and repent of sin, you agree with Satan, giving him rights in your life. Blatant rebellious sin or ongoing hidden sin can be a demonic entry point. Paul warns that if we do not properly deal with anger, it can give place to Satan, *(Ephesians 4:26-27).* If you cannot break free from sinful habits, casting out a demon may be needed.

Traumatic Experiences

Trauma can open doors for demons. Being sinned against or abused—sexually, physically, or verbally—can give demons entry into you and cause you to be bound by that traumatic experience. This trauma may cause hate, pain, and push you away from God. Various traumas and abuses open doors to demonic oppression.

Believing Demons

Satan is the father of lies; his demons speak only lies. Believing his lies means agreeing with him. He works to steal, kill, and destroy souls. When you lie about God or yourself open the door for demons to reinforce those lies in your life.

Exposure to Unholy Things

Exposure to unholy things opens demonic doors. Examples are pornography, horror movies, dark music, occult items or idols, Eight Ball, Pokémon, Dungeons and Dragons, fortune-telling, astrology, symbols of witchcraft, pagan gods or goddesses in jewelry, art, and non-Biblical religions like Yoga, Hinduism, Witchcraft, and Satanism. There are many more. There is a reason why God commands His people to come out from among the world and be holy.

Withholding Forgiveness

Bitterness, resentment, or unforgiveness towards others open doors to demons. The parable of the unmerciful servant *(Matthew 18:15-35)* ends with the unforgiving servant imprisoned and tormented. Withholding forgiveness from others puts you into a spiritual prison and gives the devil permission to torment you. It is important that you learn to choose to forgive the ones who have hurt you. This is done through the same grace that Christ gave to all of us through His Crucifixion. This does not mean that what they did was okay, and it does not mean that you cannot maintain boundaries with those who hurt you. But you must choose to walk in the same forgiveness as God has given you.

Involvement in False Religion, Cults, and Teaching

Every idol has a demon behind it *(1 Corinthians 10:19-20)*, and false teaching brings false spirits *(1 Corinthians 11:4, 1 Timothy 4:1)*. Those involved in cults or false teachings risk demonization. Whether blatant false religions like Buddhism or Hinduism, or subtle false teachings in the church, all open doors to demons.

Any Occult Involvement

Contact with the occult opens major doors to demonic influence and is forbidden in Scripture *(Deuteronomy 18:9-12)*. The occult means "secret" or "hidden" realms of Satan, including witchcraft, fortune-telling, communication with the dead, magic arts, eastern meditation, astrology, Satanism, New Age teachings, psychics, astral projection, and channeling, etc. If you have any involvement—past or present—even jokingly, verbally renounce it and seek Deliverance Ministry.

Curses

Curses, often misunderstood as superstition in the West, appear often in the Bible. Generational curses are sins or negative traits passed down through family bloodlines. Word curses involve negative speech about others. *(James 3:8-10)* warns about the tongue's power to bless and curse. *(Proverbs 18:21)* says life and death are in the power of the tongue. Some parents unknowingly curse their children with words like "You are so stupid" or "You will never amount to anything."

This list of open doors is not comprehensive. Many others exist. Many doors are open without you knowing it. When demons are cast out, it is vital to address the root causes of the problem and to make sure all doors are closed. Once closed, it is up to you to keep them closed with the Holy Spirit's help.

Signs of Demonic Intrusion

Attacks in your Dreams

Demons want to seal your peace. One of the ways they may attack you is in your sleep through sexual dreams, evil persuasion, visions of death, or visits from dead relatives or people. These are signs of demonic activity invading your sleep. "But while everyone was sleeping, his enemy came and sowed weeds and went away…" *(Matthew 13:25)*. The enemy targets your peace. Without sleep, you become restless and tired, which hampers your productivity in God's Kingdom.

Mental Oppression

Satan intrudes upon your mind with discouraging, misleading thoughts—worthlessness, failure, loneliness, confusion, and more. Your mind and emotions are the battlefield. Whether you are a believer or not, know these thoughts are NOT your own. When controlling, negative, persistent thoughts or emotions arise—unforgiveness, loneliness, self-destructive urges, a sense of powerlessness —you must declare war on them. The Bible says God gave you a sound mind. "If you do not choose to join with God to remove the root cause, the demon will infect your mind." *(2 Timothy 1:7)*.

Controlling Negative Emotions

Depression, anxiety, heaviness, rejection, resentment, unforgiveness, disappointment, loneliness, misery, self-harm, and suicidal thoughts may indicate demonic presence. These feelings are not from God. "Be anxious for nothing, but in everything by prayer and supplication, with thanksgiving, let your requests be known to God." *(Philippians 4:6)*.

"For God has not given us a spirit of fear, but of power and of love and of a sound mind." *(2 Timothy 1:7)*.

"To console those who mourn in Zion, to give them beauty for ashes, the oil of joy for mourning, the garment of praise for the spirit of heaviness; that they may be called trees of righteousness, the planting of the Lord, that He may be glorified." *(Isaiah 61:3).*

Intense Desire for Defiled Things

Demons crave the unholy and impure. Struggles with alcohol, drugs, lust, adultery, lying, stealing, or gambling are signs that something inside you craves harm. These demons often manifest through addictions or sins you cannot break. This is usually followed by shame, hatred, anger, and unforgiveness toward yourself.

You Cannot Contain Your Tongue

Being filled with the Holy Spirit enables speaking in tongues. One of the ways you can tell you are filled with demons is an impure mouth. Uncontrollable rage, cursing, gossiping, or blaspheming often indicate a demon's influence. Speaking evil about God, Christianity, or the church is a sign.

Sexual Perversion

Desires for illicit sex, masturbation, adultery, pornography, or other sexual perversions may reveal demonic influence.

Involvement In the Occult

Any spirituality that is not rooted in the Holy Bible warns of demons. Dabbling in any type of divination, tarot cards, astrology, Eight Ball, Dungeons and Dragons, Yoga, Pokémon, Harry Potter, spiritual enlightenment, etc., is an open door to demonic presence.

False Religions

Jesus said, "I am the way and the truth and the life. No one comes to the Father except through me." *(John 14:6).* False religions open you up to demons. False religion claims many paths to heaven. Jesus is the only way. Examples are Witchcraft, Masons, Eastern Star,

Satanism, Voodoo, Wicca, Hinduism, Buddhism, and worship of other gods—anything opposing Jesus' teaching.

Chronic Sickness

The Bible shows that sickness sometimes results from demons. Peter's mother had a fever Jesus rebuked, *(Matthew 8:14-15)*. The epileptic boy *(Luke 9:40-44)* and the mute boy with seizures, healed after Jesus cast out spirits *(Mark 9:17-25)*. Repeated sickness may signal a demon.

Compulsive Behavior

Sudden rage or hostility can signal demons. Saul experienced such torment and later repented *(1 Samuel 18)*.

Extreme Restlessness in Spiritual Environment

If you feel extreme tiredness while praying, reading the Bible, fasting, or worshiping, this may be a sign that demons may be present. When you grow spiritually stronger, demons try harder to stop you. *(1 Thessalonians 5:6)*.

Compulsive Desire to Hurt the Body

There was a man who was possessed by an evil spirit; he would cut himself with stones. Although the Bible states he had demons, it is also clear that they were unable to stop him from running to the feet of Jesus. His thoughts and actions were almost completely controlled, but He made a willful choice to run to Jesus. *(Mark 5:2)*. It is important to note that any thought of self-harm, harm to others, or suicide is influenced by demons.

Hearing Voices

Hearing voices referring to themselves as plural ("we," "they") or evoking fear, harm, or negativity signals demonic presence. Remember, God does not give negative feelings—demons do.

Paranormal Experiences

Supernatural events like objects disappearing, strange movements, unwarranted fear or control, noises, or other odd happenings often indicate demonic influence.

What To Do

Notice the things you are constantly led to. If you have noticed any bad or evil signs in your life, you need to sever all ties you have to that temptation or sin.

Demons are powerfully real. They cause more havoc in your life and the lives of your children than you can imagine. To counter this, you need to take God's words seriously. By knowing God, believing in and following Jesus, and being Baptized in His name, you have the power of God working with you.

The more you know God and His word, the more you will trust Him and live in obedience to Him. Strive to understand how to protect yourself and your children, so that you can defeat Satan and his demons. You can become a more dangerous threat to demons than they are to you. Listen to God, worship Him, and become more discerning about good and evil. With practice, you will learn how to take action when faced with a demonic attack.

Remember, God is light – Evil is darkness. "The God of peace will soon crush Satan under your feet. The grace of our Lord Jesus be with you." *(Romans 16:20)*.

"For those who are led by the Spirit of God are the children of God." *(Romans 8:14)*.

Pray against every demonic influence in your life. The Bible instructs you how to send devils scurrying away in fear, it says, "Submit yourselves therefore to God. Resist the devil, and he will flee from you". *(James 4:7)*.

Satan has no authority over any Christians, except the authority you grant him by allowing him into your life. This is how demons increase their influence or control over your life.

Demons recognize God's authority over them, and they tremble before it. When you submit to God, you come under His authority. You trust, obey, and follow Him. Demons do not work well in that environment, so they tend to stay away from you. This does not mean that they may not try to influence you.

You must be vigilant in your walk with God. This act of faith releases great spiritual power, and demons cannot withstand it. The more you know God and His word, the more you trust and obey Him, the more dangerous you become to Satan. *(James 2:19)*.

Deliverance Ministry is an effective way of casting out demonic influences in your life. All of this is done through the power of Jesus Christ. Negative patterns and lies are defeated by God's truth. Strongholds that have been tormenting you are broken off through the power of Jesus Christ. Without Demonic influences, you are more likely to make the right choices in your life.

Turning to God allows you to walk with Him. God will give you the knowledge, strength, and determination to overcome demonic attack in your family. God is the ultimate authority over demons and provides all the power to defeat them. Through God's Word and grace, guidance by the Holy Spirit, and salvation through Jesus Christ, you, as a believer, are empowered to overcome these evil mental, emotional, and spiritual barriers. You and your family can live a life of peace, joy, and love.

Ways to Make Demons Leave

Demons flee from God's authority, especially when you submit to God, trust Him, and obey His Word. They tremble at the name of Jesus. Your submission and faith release a holy power that demons cannot withstand.

God's Presence

Demons flee God's presence due to their fear of Christ, the power of the Holy Spirit, and the authority of God's Word. They also fear judgment and wrath and are reminded of their ultimate destination, the Abyss.

Fear Of Jesus

The Bible shows demons recognizing and fearing Jesus' authority, often fleeing at His command or when His name is mentioned. *(Mark 1:23-26; Luke 4:41).*

Demons know Christ's identity and are terrified by it. They recognize that their reign will end and the restoration Christ's presence brings. When you accept Jesus into your life, light overcomes darkness, and demons must flee.

Prayer and Authority

Prayer, especially commands spoken in Jesus' name, is a way to command demons to leave. Deliverance Ministry relies on faith, spiritual authority, and Jesus' name to command demons to leave. The demons have no choice but to leave.

Spiritual Warfare

Demons flee believers who submit to God and actively resist Satan's influence. This resistance includes standing firm in faith, relying on God's strength, actively engaging in spiritual warfare, praying, resisting evil, and wearing the Armor of God protects you and your family from demonic attack.

Demons Submit to God's Authority

Demons recognize God's authority. "You believe that God is one; you do well. Even the demons believe, and shudder!" *(James 2:19)*.

Demons are aware of God's authority and dominion over all things. Your submission to God's authority, through faith and obedience, protects you from demon influence. "Submit yourselves, then, to God. Resist the devil, and he will flee from you." *(James 4:7-8)*.

When you submit to God, are baptized, live a Christian life, accept Jesus as Lord and Savior, forgive as you have been forgiven, and depend on the Holy Spirit for guidance, you come under God's protection and forgiveness.

Trust and Obedience

Trusting and obeying God strengthens your spiritual life and makes you less vulnerable to demonic influence. Demons are opposed to God, but they recognize His authority. Your faith provides trust and obedience, which blocks demons from leading you away from God.

The Power of Prayer

With fervent, surrendered prayer, you align with God's will, releasing power from the Holy Spirit. Prayer is a powerful spiritual warfare weapon, overcoming demonic influence. Prayer calls on God's power to cast out demons and break their influence. Prayer is a form of spiritual defense, as you seek protection and deliverance from demons.

The Name of Jesus

Demons flee at Jesus' name. The power of the name lives in the authority of God's presence it represents, not just the words themselves. The name of Jesus has the power to command demons to flee. "And these signs will accompany those who believe: In my name they will cast out demons". *(Mark 16:17)*.

"She kept this up for many days. Finally Paul became so annoyed that he turned around and said to the spirit, 'In the name of Jesus Christ I command you to come out of her!' At that moment the spirit left her." *(Acts 16:18)*.

Demons Response When You Pray to God

Demons oppose your prayers to God. They see prayer as a direct threat to their efforts to block God's plan. They may try to interfere with your prayers by causing distractions or sowing doubts. But God's power is greater. Your prayers and conversations with God are powerful tools to overcome demonic oppression.

- Demons use intimidation and oppression to threaten you.
- Demons use distraction and doubt during prayers, making it difficult for you to focus on prayers to God.
- Demons try to make you think your prayers will not be answered or that God is not listening.

When you pray, demons react in various forms of opposition. They may try to disrupt or distract you, tempt you, and escalate spiritual warfare. Demons discourage prayer by projecting negative thoughts, feelings, or even physical disturbances into your life.

How Demon Interfere with Prayer

Disruption and Distraction

Demons seek to make it hard for you to focus your prayers by flooding your mind with distracting thoughts, images, or physical sensations.

Spiritual Warfare

Demons can engage in spiritual warfare by trying to manipulate or attack you through various means. They can send people, under demonic influence, to disrupt your prayers.

Seeking Openings

If you struggle with sin, you are open to demonic influence. Demons will try to exploit your vulnerability, which increases the likelihood of further demonic activity

Prayers Spoken Out Loud

Demons hear and react to your spoken or silent prayers. Remember, praying to God is stronger than any demon, and that God is always with you. You need not fear demons. Jesus' power and the Holy Spirit's protection can overcome any demonic attack. Focus on Jesus and rely on His power to overcome demonic oppression and to remain strong in your faith.

Remember, demons are constantly working to separate you and your family from God. Do not believe any negative thoughts you might have about God. God is and will always be there for you and your children. He is always prepared to listen and to guide you through life. God loves you more than you can ever imagine and wants to be a part of your life.

CHAPTER 7
Deliverance Ministry

The Bible emphasizes God as the deliverer, offering freedom from bondage and oppression—physically, emotionally, and mentally—through faith in Jesus Christ. Though not called "deliverance ministry" in Scripture, the Bible shows Jesus's power to cast out demons, break spiritual strongholds, heal the sick, and comfort people, which brings healing. This power is the foundation of deliverance ministry.

God rescues you from various forms of demonic oppression and bondage, which hinder spiritual growth and obedience to God. One way this is accomplished is through the Deliverance Ministry. Spiritual healing is available to each of us, as shown in Jesus' ministry. Jesus, through His teachings and actions, emphasizes deliverance from sin, spiritual bondage, physical afflictions, and even death. Through faith in Jesus Christ and the Power of the Holy Spirit, Deliverance offers freedom and healing.

God As the Deliverer

Jesus' ministry includes healing the sick and casting out demons, demonstrating His authority over evil spirits and His power to deliver people from bondage.

Authority in Jesus' Name

The New Testament stresses the authority believers receive in Jesus' name, including the power to cast out demons.

Deliverance as a Spiritual Concept

Deliverance ministry focuses on spiritual freedom from sin and restoring a relationship with God, and physical, mental, and emotional healing, through the power of Jesus Christ.

Distinction from Exorcism

Exorcism targets demonic possession and is designed for unbelievers. Deliverance ministry can address demonic possession, but usually addresses demonic oppression. It is primarily used by baptized Christians. Both cast out demons through the power of Jesus Christ.

Bible Basis

The Bible provides examples and principles supporting the Deliverance Ministry. Such as prayer, the power and authority of Jesus's name, and the role of the Holy Spirit.

Jesus Deliverance from Sin and Bondage

Jesus preached the Gospel, performed miracles, healed the sick and brokenhearted, raised the dead, and set Satan's captives free. He sacrificed Himself for humanity's sins, so that we can achieve salvation.

Power of the Holy Spirit

Through the power of the Holy Spirit and Jesus' holy name, Christians are empowered to cast out demons and to overcome negative influences.

Repentance and Alignment with God

Jesus calls you to repent and experience freedom, turning from sin and aligning with God's will.

Faith in Jesus Christ

Through faith in Jesus, you experience deliverance and the freedom only God provides.

Signs of Belief

Jesus states believers will show signs like casting out demons, speaking in tongues, healing, and receiving spiritual gifts to serve others.

Resisting the Devil

Jesus' teachings encourage believers to resist the devil by submitting to God, having faith in Jesus, and relying on God's Word.

Jesus as the Ultimate Deliverer

As the Ultimate Deliverer, Jesus frees you from sin, bondage, and spiritual oppression.

Freedom in Christ

Jesus' sacrifice on the Cross is the ultimate deliverance act, freeing you from sin's penalty and darkness's power.

Deliverance from Eternal Punishment

Jesus rescues you from "wrath to come" and gives eternal life to believers.

Deliverance Ministries

Deliverance ministry helps you receive the life God intends you to have. Be desperate, Christ, and believe in the delivering power of Jesus Christ.

Deliverance ministry frees you from demonic influence and sin through Jesus' name and the Holy Spirit, received at baptism.

Deliverance ministry casts out demons, helping you overcome spiritual strongholds—negative behaviors, feelings, emotions, and experiences—leading to freedom and closer fellowship with God, enabling better ministry to others.

Baptized Christians cannot be demonically possessed but can be oppressed by demons. This means demons can influence and persuade you away from God by affecting your mind, body, and emotions. Baptized Christians have the ability to be helped and guided by the Holy Spirit. He helps you to receive the gifts of Deliverance through the power of Jesus Christ, which provides a new step in your journey of faith in Jesus as your Lord and Savior.

Non-Christians, who have not been baptized and have not accepted Jesus as their Savior, can be demonically possessed —affected physically, mentally, emotionally, and spiritually. Because they have not accepted Jesus as their Lord and Savior and have not been baptized, a non-believer or an unbaptized person can find it much harder to achieve a good result at Deliverance.

Another facet of Deliverance Ministry is to help guide you by means of expressions of faith, repentance, forgiveness, breaking generational curses and soul ties, etc. This gives people a way to offer repentance to God for sin and receive forgiveness from God. Deliverance offers the opportunity for a new relationship with God, family, and friends.

Note:

Unfortunately, not all Deliverance Ministries are the same. Some are untrained, some are only interested in the money they charge, some really do not have your best interest at heart, and some just make it up as they go along. While others are truly servants of God. They are only interested in doing His will, following methods and practices that have been utilized over the centuries of the Church. God the Father, Jesus, and the Holy Spirit are the heart of their ministry. They depend on the Bible for guidance. Helping others find freedom is the most important goal. When you choose a Deliverance Ministry, it is wise to get counsel from others or your Pastor, who has experience with that ministry.

Note:

Deliverance Ministry is different from Healing Ministry. Healing ministry primarily refers to the restoration of the physical, emotional, and spiritual body through prayer and intercession. Deliverance Ministry refers to the casting out of demons through the power of Jesus Christ and the help of the Holy Spirit. Deliverance Ministry can help free people from torment, bondage, and oppression, as God the Father continues His steadfast love and protection for you. Deliverance is not a power encounter; it is a faith encounter.

Spiritual Warfare Through the Bible and Prayer

According to Paul, all of life is spiritual warfare. He tells you in Ephesians how important it is and that the Armor of God alone is not enough. You need to stay in constant contact with God through prayer, *(Ephesians 6:18-20)*. The Bible encourages prayer as a way to fight spiritual warfare and to access the resources God provides.

Bible Verses for Spiritual Warfare Prayer

- "No weapon forged against you will prevail." *(Isaiah 54:17)*.
- "For though we live in the world, we do not wage war as the world does. The weapons we fight with are not the weapons of the world." *(2 Corinthians 10:3-5)*.
- "He who dwells in the shelter of the Most High will abide in the shadow of the Almighty." *(Psalm 91)*.
- "Submit yourselves therefore to God. Resist the devil, and he will flee from you." *(James 4:7)*.
- "No weapon forged against you will prevail, and you will refute every tongue that accuses you." *(Isaiah 54:17)*.
- "Do not be anxious about anything, but in every situation, by prayer and petition, with thanksgiving, present your requests to God." *(Philippians 4:6-7)*.

Prayer Statements for Spiritual Warfare

- "Strengthen my faith, Lord. Forgive my sins, so that I may be clean in your righteousness."
- "Give me your wisdom and discernment so I will not be caught off guard."
- "Help me to avoid temptation and deliver me from evil, Lord."

- "I declare and decree that I am more than a conqueror through Jesus Christ."
- "I come to Your refuge with joy for You shelter me against the attack of the devil."
- "I invite you to fill me afresh today, and have complete control over my life."
- "I claim in every way Your victory over all satanic forces active in my life."
- "I am thankful, Heavenly Father, that the weapons of our warfare are not carnal but mighty through God to the pulling down of strongholds, to the casting down of imaginations and every high thing that exalts itself against the knowledge of God, and to bring every thought into obedience to the Lord Jesus Christ."

Prayer for Intercession

"Heavenly Father, I come before You today, acknowledging the spiritual battles I face. I stand firm in Your power and authority, clothed in the full Armor of God: the belt of truth, the breastplate of righteousness, the shield of faith, the helmet of salvation, and the sword of the Spirit, which is Your Word. I declare that no weapon formed against me shall prosper, and I resist every attack of the enemy in Jesus' name. I strengthen my faith. Give me discernment to recognize the schemes of Satan. Empower me to stand against every stronghold of darkness. Lord, I ask for Your protection over me and my loved ones. I submit my will to Yours. Thank You for providing Your victory over evil and for the assurance that I am more than a conqueror through Christ Jesus. Amen."

Prayer for Victory

"Heavenly Father, I come before You today with a heart overflowing with gratitude and praise. You are the Almighty God, the Lord of Hosts, my Defender, and my Deliverer. Thank You for the victory You have secured for me through Jesus Christ, my Savior and King. Lord, I praise You because in every battle, You have been my strength. When Satan came in like a flood, You lifted a standard against him. When I felt weak and weary, Your Spirit empowered me to stand firm in faith. Thank You for breaking every chain that once held me captive and for tearing down strongholds that sought to keep me bound. Amen."

Prayer of Thanksgiving

"I declare, Lord, that the weapons of my warfare are not carnal, but mighty through You. You pull down every stronghold of fear, doubt, and sin. Thank You for arming me with the belt of truth, the shield of faith, and the sword of the Spirit. Through Your Word, I have overcome the schemes of Satan and have walked in the freedom Christ purchased for me at the cross. Father, I thank You that no weapon formed against me shall prosper. Thank You for teaching my hands to war and my fingers to fight, for guiding me with wisdom, and for surrounding me with Your angels of protection.

"Lord, today I stand victorious, not by my own might or power, but by Your Spirit. Thank You for the breakthroughs, the deliverance, and the restoration You have brought into my life. I want to be more than a conqueror through Christ, who loves me. May my life always reflect Your glory, and may I walk boldly in the authority You have given me. Help me to remain steadfast, watchful, and clothed in Your righteousness, knowing that You who have begun a good work in me will help me carry it to completion. All honor, glory, and praise belong to You, Lord. In Jesus' mighty name, I give thanks and declare victory over evil. Amen."

Other Tips for Spiritual Warfare

Put God first

Stay close to Jesus

Look to the Holy Spirit to unite you with Christ

Empower Christian living

Guide you in truth and comfort

Pray and listen for God's direction in your life

Read the Bible daily

Know the real enemy

Put on the full Armor of God

Submit to God and resist the Devil

Invoke the authority of Jesus

Live out your true identity

Spiritual Warfare for Your Family

Satan knows God created marriage as a beautiful, living picture of Christ and the Church. God designed marriage and family for your benefit. Satan knows the value of the family as the base of society, the foundation of the Church, and the future of God's work on earth. Should Satan become successful in tearing down the structure of the family, he will be successful in damaging what is loved by God.

Satan Attacks the Foundation of the Family – Marriage

When God created the first couple, He called it "very good." Adam and Eve were united in a holy bond before God. God said, "Therefore a man shall leave his father and his mother and hold fast to his wife, and they shall become one flesh." *(Genesis 2:24)* God requires a married couple to separate from others and to make a commitment to each other. This commitment is a stable foundation for the family unit.

Satan's initial attack on the family occurred in Eden, where the serpent worked his evil deception on Eve and destroyed the harmony of the first marriage. When Eve and Adam listened to the serpent and disobeyed God, they were banished from the Garden. "So the Lord God banished him from the Garden of Eden to work the ground from which he had been taken. After he drove the man out, he placed on the east side of the Garden of Eden cherubim and a flaming sword flashing back and forth to guard the way to the tree of life." *(Genesis 3:23-24)*.

Because of Adam and Eve's sin, all future families inherited God's judgment. Today, the increasing rate of divorce, immorality, abortion, and same-gender marriage in society shows pervasive sin. Satan is very good at twisting God's Word to pervert families to sin and deny the blessings of a holy marriage.

Satan's Attack on the Family Unit

Good marriages were the foundation of solid families. If Satan can successfully destroy the marriage, this will have a destructive impact on the rest of the family. At least 85% of children with behavioral disorders come from fatherless homes. Our society shifts from a cohesive family unit to merely living together, increasing family instability.

Understanding God's design helps you recognize Satan's attempts to change and undermine it. Paul and Peter give clear instructions about family responsibility and authority in (*Ephesians 5:22, Ephesians 6:4, Colossians 3:18-21, 1 Timothy 5:14, Titus 2:4-5, and 1 Peter 3:1-7*). Two enduring truths that appear in these passages are the husband's headship and the wife's submission.

The Bible equates a husband and wife's relationship to that of Christ and the Church. Husband, through Christ-like leadership, assumes the responsibility of protection and provision in the home. The husband is to love his wife and to give himself up to her, as Christ loves the Church. He is to nourish and cherish her. The wife is to submit to her husband, who is living out the responsibility God has given him. She has the divine calling of a wife and mother. This means to honor and affirm her husband's leadership and to help carry it through, according to her own gift from God. The husband is to love his wife "as Christ loved the Church and gave Himself up for her," and to "nourish and cherish" her as one would his own body. This is why the husband is called to provide godly leadership through sacrificial love. The wife is to respect her loving husband. Then the marriage will flourish. The husband, who is fulfilling his role as head of his home, will put the needs of his family first. Then the wife is able to feel secure in the love and devotion of her husband and will support and help him in every possible way.

Satan distorts these divine mandates from God – leadership and submission. Some men control their wives and families for self-serving reasons; some abdicate responsibility. Some women are dominated by their husbands, while other women seek to be the controlling force in the family and do not respect their husbands. In these relationships, Satan has been very successful in persuading men and women to abandon God's plan.

Rejecting godly headship and submission harms your family and makes it less than it should be. Satan has been successful at his evil work of deception. Pray God grants husbands courage to lead lovingly, and wives the grace to respect and support their husbands.

The Bible provides clear guidelines for the children's place in family life. God instructs them to obey their parents. "Children, obey your parents in the Lord, for this is right. Honor your father and mother." *(Ephesians 6:1-2)*. Satan and his demons undermine parental authority in the home. This will introduce messages of disobedience to your child. He seeks to reduce the parents' ability to assert their authority over the children. through media, music, and the internet, promoting disobedience. Fathers are portrayed as weak; music encourages rebellion. All of this sets up demons to whisper that submission and obedience are not good for them. The atmosphere of the home are important parental responsibilities. If fathers are to bring up children in the "discipline and instruction of the Lord," they must fulfill their leadership responsibilities in the family. This is to be done lovingly, without provoking their children to anger. *(Ephesians 6:4)*. Mothers love, nurture, and guide in harmony with husbands to make the home safe, loving, and godly.

Satan Attacks The Intention of God in Your Home

Home is where God's Word is taught, where healthy godly principles are explained and lived out in the daily life of your family. Timothy's life of faith began in his grandmother's and mother's homes. "Continue in what you have learned and become convinced of... from infancy you have known the Holy Scriptures, which make you wise for salvation through faith in Christ." *(2 Timothy 3:15)*.

Make the Bible a home priority in your home, because God's Word is the necessary foundation for all families. Today, many families are so busy that they have little time to read the Bible, let alone study it and put it into practice in your life. Spending time in God's Word and waiting on Him is essential. If Satan can keep families too busy for the Bible, they can lose their joy, strength, and effectiveness in this world.

Husbands and wives need time alone to nurture their relationship. They need time with their children, if you are going to fulfill the Biblical mandate of training up a child in the way he should go. *(Proverbs 22:6)*. Time with your children and focusing on them are lost when the family members' lives become frantically busy and stressed. The family needs time when all electronic equipment, Internet, and telephone are off so that the needs of your family can be lovingly met. Time must be taken for reading and praying together and for eating and playing together. By following God's plan, He will be glorified and your family will be blessed.

When parents walk with God and follow His Word, Christlike attitudes and behaviors emerge, drawing children's hearts to God. Without the fruit of the Spirit—love, joy, peace, patience, kindness, goodness, faithfulness, gentleness, self-control—the family suffers loss. Satan's seeds of unforgiveness destroy peace, joy, and integrity; distorted truth erodes trust and causes damage. Your family's ultimate defense is living in God's truth and love.

Ways To Fight Back For Your Family

Be A Prayer Warrior

Too many parents pray only when problems arise. Parents who pray regularly for their children's minds, because their thoughts determine their choices. That is why every parent needs to be a prayer warrior for their child.

Each of your children needs prayer for specific things in their lives. These prayers should be supported by the Bible. Such as do not pray that your son wins the ballgame. Pray that he displays a godly attitude in both winning and losing. Pray those things with your children so they understand what is most important to God.

Ways to Pray for School-Age Children:

- Pray for their teachers and administrators regularly.
- Pray that school is a spiritual battleground. Instead of being scared about what your children are facing each day, be active in it through prayer.
- Ask principals and teachers how you can pray for them and their classrooms. If they are unsure, be ready to pray for them specifically.
- Pray now for your children to have godly friends.

Pray daily for your spouse and your marriage—demons want to disrupt your home. If they cannot destroy your family, they will settle for anger and conflict. Satan does not want godly parents for children.

For effective prayers, confess and repent your own personal sins. Ask God's forgiveness and grace. Ask for forgiveness from your children if your words or actions have not reflected Christ.

Be A Teacher

You are responsible for teaching your children truth from God's Word. This is not just about keeping evil out, it is about putting righteousness in. God answers all your questions and those of your children about life and culture. The Bible tells you and your children how to respond and what attitudes to have. Remember, you are their primary teacher.

If you feel you do not know enough about the Bible, just read it. You do not have to know all the answers; you just have to be willing to learn.

Be An Example

Children learn about God by watching you. You can send them to a Christian school, but they can get confused if they do not see at home what they see at school. Wholehearted obedience to God includes refusing evil, even in your entertainment. It refuses to tolerate or participate in anything God calls evil, including your own entertainment choices.

Be an Obstacle

Spiritual warfare surrounds your family, as well as other families. You are called on to stand as an obstacle to Satan. Be engaging and an enthusiastic supporter in your children's lives—know their games, music, books, and interests.

Be a Prayer Warrior

Pray for your children daily, not only for their needs, but also for protection, discernment, and their spiritual growth.

Examples:

"Lord, I want to be more passionate that my children know You and grow in You, than about anything else."

"Lord, protect my children from all harm, and Holy Spirit watch over them and guide them through their day."

Your children deserve devoted, godly parents. Demons should have to crawl over you to get to your children. Be a prayer warrior in your church family. Help other families as they pray for their children. Stand for righteousness. If demons seek to steal, kill, and destroy your children and grandchildren, they must come through you first!

God created the family, providing divine design and instruction in Scripture for your family to flourish. Know Satan's patterns to spot subtle patterns of attacks. Let the fruit of the Spirit—love, joy, peace, patience, kindness, goodness, faithfulness, gentleness, self-control—characterize your family's life. You need godly leadership, respect, love, prayer, as well as dependence on God. He alone can preserve your family. He loves you and your children and wants the best for you all.

"Dear Lord, help families follow Your truth and cling closely to You." Amen

Pray Guidance and Protection over Yourself and Your Family

To Be Read Aloud:

Heavenly Father,

I bow in worship and praise before You. I cover myself with the blood of the Lord Jesus Christ as my protection. I surrender myself completely in every area of my life to You. I take a stand against all the workings of Satan that would hinder me in my prayer life. You are the only True and Living God. I refuse any involvement of Satan in my life and prayers. I command Satan, in the Name of the Lord Jesus Christ, to leave my presence with all of his demons. Holy Spirit, bring the blood of the Lord Jesus Christ between Satan and my family. Amen

Heavenly Father,

I worship You and give You praise. I recognize that You are worthy to receive all glory and honor and praise. I renew my commitment to You and pray that the Holy Spirit will enable me during this time of prayer. I am thankful, Heavenly Father, that You have loved me from the beginning and that You sent the Lord Jesus Christ into the world to die for my sins. I am thankful that Jesus came as my Savior and that through Him I am completely forgiven. You have adopted me into Your family; You have assumed all responsibility for me. You have given me eternal life. I am thankful that through Jesus, You have made me complete, and that You have offered Yourself to me and my family to be my daily help and strength. Amen

Heavenly Father,

Open my eyes that I might see how great You are and how complete Your provision is for this day. I am thankful for the victory Jesus Christ won for me on the Cross. In His Resurrection, faith and salvation have been given to me. I am thankful I am a child of God.

I take my place as God's child. Through my faith, baptism, and the presence of the Holy Spirit, I declare that Satan and his demons have no hold on me and are subject to our Lord Jesus Christ. I am thankful for the Armor You have provided. I put on the Belt of Truth, the Breastplate of Righteousness, the Shoes of Peace, and the Helmet of Salvation. I lift the Shield of Faith against all evil. I take in my hand the Sword of the Spirit, the Word of God. I choose to use Your Word against all the forces of evil in my life. I put on this Armor and live and pray in complete dependence upon You. I am grateful, Heavenly Father, that Jesus Christ triumphed over all demonic principalities and powers. I claim all that victory for my life today. I reject all the insinuations, accusations, lies, and temptations of Satan. I affirm that the Word of God is true, and I choose to live today in the light of God's Word. I choose to live in obedience to You, Father. I choose to worship You as my loving almighty God. Open my eyes and show me the areas of my life that do not please You. Work in me to cleanse me from all sin that would give Satan a foothold against me. I do stand as Your adopted child, and I welcome all the ministry of the Holy Spirit. By faith and dependence upon You, I stand in all the victory of the Resurrection and the provision Jesus Christ has given me to live above sin. Therefore, today I take off the sinful nature with its selfishness and pride. I put on the new nature with its love. I take off the old nature with its fear, and I put on the new nature with its courage. I take off the old nature with its weakness and I put on the new nature with its strength. I take off the old nature with all its deceitful lusts, and I put on the new nature with its righteousness, purity, and honesty. In every way, I stand in the victory of the Death, Burial, and Resurrection of my Lord Jesus Christ. I claim my place in Christ as victorious with Him over all the enemies of my soul. Holy Spirit, I pray that You would fill me. Come into my life, break down every idol and cast out every demon, and guide and direct me in the ways of God. Amen

Heavenly Father,

I am thankful for the expression of Your will in my daily life. As You have shown me in Your Word, I claim the will of God for me today. I am thankful that You have blessed me with all spiritual blessings through Christ Jesus. I am thankful that You have made me a living hope by the resurrection of Jesus Christ from the dead. I am thankful that You have provided for me today, so I can live filled with the Spirit of God, with love, joy, and peace, long suffering, gentleness and goodness, meekness, faithfulness, and self-control in my life. I recognize that this is Your will for me, and I reject and resist all the endeavors of Satan and his demons to rob me of the will of God. I refuse to believe my feelings. I hold up the shield of faith against all the accusations, distortions, insinuations, and lies that Satan would put into my mind. I claim the will of God for my life today. In the Name of the Lord Jesus Christ, I completely surrender myself to You, Heavenly Father, as a living sacrifice. I choose not to be conformed to this world. I choose to be transformed by the renewing of my mind, and I pray that You would show me Your will and enable me to walk in all the fullness of Your will today. Amen

Heavenly Father,

I am thankful that the weapons of our warfare are mighty through God, to pull down strongholds, to cast down every high thing that exalts above God, and to bring every thought into obedience to the Lord Jesus Christ. Therefore, in my own life today, I tear down the strongholds of Satan and smash the plans of Satan that have been formed against me. I tear down the strongholds of Satan against my mind, my emotions, and my body, and I surrender them all to You. I affirm, Heavenly Father, that You have not given me the spirit of fear but of power and of love and of a sound mind. I break and smash the strongholds of Satan formed against my emotions today, and I give my emotions to You. I smash the strongholds of Satan formed against my mind today, I give my will to You, and choose to make the right decisions of faith. I smash the strongholds of Satan formed against my body today. I give my body to You, recognizing that I am Your temple. I rejoice in Your mercy and goodness. Amen

CHAPTER 8

Cleanse Your Home of Demonic Influence

As a believer in Christ, through the power of the Holy Spirit, you have authority over demons. By prayer, anointing, and cleansing, you can make your home a peaceful, holy place where God's presence dwells. Be diligent in spiritual house cleaning, anointing, and prayer, trusting God to protect and bless your home.

Spiritual house cleansing as understood through the Bible includes prayer, seeking God's protection, and casting out demons. Key passages include:

"But when the Pharisees heard this, they said, 'It is only by Beelzebul, the prince of demons, that this fellow drives out demons.'" *(Matthew 12:43-45).*

"When an impure spirit comes out of a person, it goes through arid places seeking rest and does not find it. Then it says, 'I will return to the house I left.'" *(Luke 11:24).*

"Whoever dwells in the shelter of the Most High will rest in the shadow of the Almighty. I will say of the Lord, "He is my refuge and my fortress, my God, in whom I trust." Surely he will save you from the fowler's snare and from the deadly pestilence. He will cover you with his feathers, and under his wings you will find refuge; his faithfulness will be your shield and rampart. You will not fear the terror of night, nor the arrow that flies by day, nor the pestilence that stalks in the darkness, nor the plague that destroys at midday. A thousand may fall at your side, ten thousand at your right hand, but it will not come near you. You will only observe with your eyes and see the punishment of the wicked. If you say, "The Lord is my refuge," and you make the Most High your dwelling, no harm will overtake you, no disaster will come near your tent. For he will command his angels concerning you to guard you in all your ways; they will lift you up in their hands, so that you will not strike your foot against a stone. You will tread on the lion and the cobra; you will trample the great lion and the serpent. "Because he loves me," says the Lord, "I will rescue him; I will protect him, for he acknowledges my name. He will call on me, and I will answer him; I will be with him in trouble, I will deliver him and honor him. With long life I will satisfy him and show him my salvation." *(Psalm 91).*

Ways To Tell If There Is A Demonic Influence In Your Home

- You have no peace. Everyone is fighting and at odds with each other
- You sense something is not right.
- Someone returned from a trip and unknowingly brought back a demonic object.
- Presence of pornography in the home.
- Spiritual attacks occur at home.
- After watching or reading something on TV, or any other kind of media or books, you feel a disturbing presence. Something is not quite right.
- A changed atmosphere when visitors come or leave your home.
- A person in the home is practicing witchcraft, Santeria, or pagan religions.
- A family member is emotionally bound.

Remove Entertainment That Pollutes Your Home

Be careful about what you allow in your home under the guise of entertainment. Some people may say, "It's just a movie." Or "It's only TV, we all know it is not real. Young children do not know if it is real or not. It is not just entertainment. TV programming programs our minds. Entertainment can be very, very wicked. Would you allow someone to come into your house and blaspheme the name of the Lord, as entertainment does? We cannot un-see the evil once we have taken it in with our eyes and ears. Use discernment with entertainment, as well as all the objects permitted in your home.

Look for non-Christian items inside and outside related to evil, the occult, or Satan. Such as art, books, magazines, music, decor, jewelry, clothing, games, Internet chat rooms, etc. All of these are considered "Open Doors", which are ways Satan and his demons enter or return to your life and home. Should you find anything, you should destroy it by fire or discard such items immediately so others will not stumble upon it. Remove anything demonic or dark; only light belongs in your home.

House Cleansing Prayers

Christian house cleansing and consecration prayers are powerful ways to spiritually cleanse, consecrate, and bless your home. As you pray, walk through each room. While praying out loud, you can use anointing oil or blessed water to draw a cross on all of the doors and windows. This action symbolizes the protection of God, as demonstrated at the time of Moses, as well as Jesus Christ, our Savior and Lord. You can incorporate scripture readings into your cleansing prayers. Do not use sage or any other substance, symbol, or device that is used in non-Christian rites.

A Christian House cleansing prayer can be a powerful way to spiritually cleanse and bless your home. This housecleaning prayer can be repeated if needed.

"Father, thank You for blessing and provision of this home. Thank you that you have given me authority to trample on every power of the enemy, authority to bind and loose and to release the atmosphere of heaven on earth. Amen *(Luke 10:19, Matthew 6:10, Matthew 16:19)*.

"Right now, in the name of Jesus Christ, I take full authority over this home. I renounce all ungodliness and all sinful activity that has ever taken place in this home. I renounce the sin of all previous owners, renters, guests, and builders. Any curses or evil agreements ever made in or over this home, I now declare broken, null, and void in the name and authority of Jesus. In the name of Jesus, I also command every unclean spirit to be bound and to leave my home right now. In the name of Jesus Christ, I cancel every claim and right the enemy might have here. In the name of Jesus Christ, I cleanse this home and everything in it. In the name of Jesus Christ, I command any and all demons to leave this home and take any negativity, darkness, or unholy influences with you. I invite the Holy Spirit to fill this home with Your presence, love, and peace. I dedicate this house to You, Lord, and ask that it be a place of joy, healing, and blessing. I thank you for your faithfulness and protection. Jesus, I ask that you will also send your angels to cleanse this home now, to establish your kingdom here, and to build a shield of protection around this home. I ask you to guard all who enter or leave this home. Let nothing enter this house that is not of you. Amen"

Pay close attention to rooms where you have sensed conflict, discomfort, or spiritual heaviness. Be sure and command any lingering demonic spirits to leave in Jesus' name. Use prayers that focus on rebuking evil and inviting God's presence into your home. Declare that you and your family are loved by God, empowered by Jesus Christ, and that your home is a dwelling place of the Holy Spirit.

Prayer for Protection:

"Dear Heavenly Father,

In Jesus' mighty name, we come to You. We ask for Your divine protection over us. Drive away any disruptive spirits or demons. Surround us with Your angels and grant us Your peace. Help us stand strong in You, wearing the full Armor of God daily. In Jesus' name, Amen."

Bless Your Home

House Blessing

You can bless your house alone or with family and friends. Walk through each room, making the sign of the cross over windows and doors with oil or water. At each main doorway, pray one or more prayers. Use either oil or water for anointing.

Blessing Oil or Water for Spiritual Protection

Use blessed oil or water to anoint each room in the house. Blessed oil and water involve seeking God's power and presence in these elements. They have long been used as symbols of God's power and presence for healing, protection, and cleansing.

Blessing Oil

Father, I humbly come before you to ask for your blessing upon this water. I ask that you fill it with Your divine power and presence, that it may be a conduit of Your grace and protection. I dedicate this water for protection and spiritual strengthening. I pray that wherever it is used, it will bring forth Your blessings. May this water be a source of strength and protection for this family, and may it be a reminder of your grace and love. I ask this in the name of our Lord and Savior, Jesus Christ. Amen

Blessing Water

"Father, I humbly come before you to ask for your blessing upon this water. I ask that you fill it with Your divine power and presence, that it may be a conduit of Your grace and protection. I dedicate this water for protection and spiritual strengthening. I pray that wherever it is used, it will bring forth Your blessings. May this water be a source of strength and protection for this family, and may it be a reminder of your grace and love. I ask this in the name of our Lord and Savior, Jesus Christ. Amen. "

"Come, Holy Spirit. Come and fill every part of this home with the fullness of the kingdom of God, with your love, your peace, and your rest. May Your Holy Spirit flow through and fill this home up with Your Spirit. Amen

"Lord, bless me, my family, and friends coming through this door. Lord bless delivery persons doing their jobs, any strangers, rich or poor. Help me welcome everyone and pass along Your peace, and whether I'm coming or going, may my love for you increase". Amen

"Let us now pray that the Holy Spirit will enter this home and bless it with His presence. May He always be here among us; may He nurture our love for each other, share in our joys, and comfort us in our sorrows. We pray this in the name of Jesus, our Lord."

Request Protection

"Lord Jesus,
in Your love and mercy to establish a perimeter of protection around my family, myself, and all our loved ones. I ask that the Holy Angels guard us and all our possessions, and this property, rendering us immune from any kind of demonic influence. I ask that no demonic bondage, door, demonic entity, portal, astral projection, or disembodied spirit may enter the property in any direction. I ask You to send us your Angels to protect us from harm, including any demon interference or involvement within the vicinity of our property. I ask that should demons try to enter, they are prevented by your Angels. That You will strip them of all weapons and authority. Amen."

Prayer for Binding Demons

"Lord Jesus,
In your Holy Name, I ask you to bind up any demonic forces from manifesting on our property. In Your Holy Name, I ask you to

remove any demons or demon attachments from our property. Amen"

"In Jesus' name,

I bind all spirits in the air, and the fire and the water, in the ground and the underground. I bind any satanic forces of nature," I command any unclean thing that is not of you to leave immediately in Jesus' name. Amen"

"Lord Jesus,

I ask You to render all spirits impotent, paralyzed, and ineffective in attempting to take revenge against me, my family, my friends, my community, and those who pray for me and my family. I ask You to bind all evil spirits, all powers of the air, the water, the ground, the fire, underground, or wherever they exercise their powers, any satanic forces in nature, and any and all emissaries of the satanic headquarters. I ask You to bind, by Your Precious Blood, all of the attributes, aspects and characteristics, interactions, communications and deceitful games of demons. I ask You to break any and all bonds, ties, and attachments. Amen."

Prayers for Protection Over Your Property

To pray for the protection of your yard from demons, focus on seeking God's power and presence, invoking angels, and rebuking evil influences. You can use specific prayers, like the one from *"Exodus 90"*, which asks for a perimeter of protection around you and your loved ones, including the yard. You can also use *"Psalm 91"*, which speaks of God's refuge and protection.

"Lord Jesus,

In Your love and mercy to establish a perimeter of protection around my family, myself, and all our loved ones. I ask that the Holy Angels guard us and all our possessions, and this property, rendering us immune from any kind of demonic influence. I ask that no demonic bondage, door, demonic entity, portal, astral projection, or disembodied spirit may enter the property in any direction. I ask You to send us your Angels to protect us from harm, including any demon interference or involvement within the vicinity of our property. I ask that, should demons try to enter, they are prevented by your Angels. That You will strip them of all weapons and authority. That You will bind, rebuke, and disable them from communicating or interacting with each other or with us. Please remove them, sending them directly to the Abyss. All this I ask in Your Holy Name. Amen"

"Heavenly Father,

I come before you today, seeking Your guidance and protection for this home. I ask that you cleanse this space of any negativity, darkness, or unholy influences. I command any evil spirits or forces to leave this home in the name of Jesus. I invite your Holy Spirit to fill this home with your presence, love, and peace. I dedicate this house to you, Lord, and ask that it be a place of joy, healing, and blessing. I thank you for your faithfulness and protection. Amen."

"Lord Jesus,

You are the Head of my household. I invite Your authority and dominion to reign over this place. Through the name power of Your name, I bind every demon and cast them into the abyss. Through the name of Jesus Christ, I command that no demonic forces are permitted to operate or linger here." Amen

"Heavenly Father,

I come before you asking for Your presence and protection in this home. I ask that you cleanse this space of evil influences or spiritual disturbances. May Your holy light shine brightly in every corner of every room, filling it with Your love and peace. I pray that You surround this home, and all who dwell within it, with Your divine protection. Guard us from all harm, both seen and unseen, and keep us safe from any spiritual attacks. I ask that you bless this home and all who enter it, that they may feel Your presence and experience Your peace. In the name of Jesus Christ, I command all demons to leave this home. Thank you, Jesus, for cleansing and purifying this home. Thank you, Lord, for your constant presence and protection. Through the protection of the Holy Spirit and Your angels, may this home be a sanctuary of peace, love, and joy, where Your name is honored and Your will be done. Amen"

Consecrate Your Home and Property to God

Consecration means the separation of anything that is unclean, especially anything that would contaminate your relationship with God. Consecration also has the meaning of sanctification, holiness, or purity. It means to dedicate or set apart yourself and your belongings to the service and worship of God.

It can also be a personal commitment to living a life that is holy and pleasing to God, often involving a separation from worldly pursuits and a focus on spiritual growth and service.

Consecration and Dedication Prayers

A prayer of consecration is a prayer where someone dedicates themselves or something to God's service and purposes, setting it apart as holy. It's a deliberate act of surrendering oneself or possessions to God's will, often with the intention of living a life aligned with His purposes. This can involve dedicating one's time, talents, or even physical possessions to God's work.

Heavenly Father,

I now consecrate and dedicate this home and the land it is on to the rule of Jesus, the presence of the Holy Spirit, and the Kingdom of God. I dedicate everything in and around this house to the Lord Jesus and claim that it is under His rule, protection. I ask Your blessing in every room and everything within it. Come, Holy Spirit, and fill every part of this home with the fullness of the kingdom of God, with your love, your peace, and your rest. Jesus, I ask that You would also send Your angels to cleanse this home now, to establish Your kingdom here, and to build a shield of protection around it. In the mighty name of The Lord Jesus Christ, I now proclaim that this home, land, and everything in it is property of the Kingdom of God. Amen"

Ongoing Prayers

"Lord, I invite Your authority and dominion to reign over this place. Through the power of Your name, I bind every spiritual enemy and cast them far from these premises. I command that no demonic forces are permitted to operate or linger here. Establish Your kingdom rule, and let angelic guards surround and protect this home."

"Come, Holy Spirit. come and fill every part of this home with the fullness of the kingdom of God, with your love, your peace, and your rest. Jesus, I ask that you would also send your angels to cleanse this home now, to establish your kingdom here, and to build a shield of protection around it. In the mighty name of Jesus Christ the Lord, I now proclaim that his home, land, and everything in it is property of the Kingdom of God."

Spiritual Warfare Scriptures

The concept of "God reading the word" refers to the idea that God's Word, often understood as the Bible, is a living and active force, a source of divine truth and guidance, and a reflection of God's character and will.

"Submit yourselves to God. Resist the devil, and he will flee from you." *(James 4:7)*.

"You are from God, little children, and have overcome them; because greater is He who is in you than he who is in the world." *(1 John 4:4)*.

"For though we live in the world, we do not wage war as the world does. The weapons we fight with are not the weapons of the world. On the contrary, they have divine power to demolish strongholds. We demolish arguments and every pretension that sets itself up against the knowledge of God, and we take captive every thought to make it obedient to Christ." *(2 Corinthians 10:3-5).*

"Be self-controlled and alert. Your enemy the devil prowls around like a roaring lion looking for someone to devour. Resist him, standing firm in the faith." *(1 Peter. 5:8-9).*

"No weapon that is formed against you will prosper; and every tongue that accuses you in judgment you will condemn. This is the heritage of the servants of the Lord, and their vindication is from Me," declares the Lord." *(Isaiah 54:17).*

Put on the full armor of God, so that you can take your stand against the devil's schemes. For our struggle is not against flesh and blood, but against the rulers, against the authorities, against the powers of this dark world and against the spiritual forces of evil in the heavenly realms. Therefore put on the full armor of God, so that when the day of evil comes, you may be able to stand your ground, and after you have done everything, to stand. Stand firm then, with the belt of truth buckled around your waist, with the breastplate of righteousness in place, and with your feet fitted with the readiness that comes from the gospel of peace. In addition to all this, take up the shield of faith, with which you can extinguish all the flaming arrows of the evil one. Take the helmet of salvation and the sword of the Spirit, which is the word of God." *(Ephesians 6:11-17).*

"In all these things, we are more than conquerors through Him who loved us." *(Romans 8:37).*

"But thanks be to God, who gives us the victory through our Lord Jesus Christ" *(1 Corinthians 15:57).*

"Not by might nor by power, but by My Spirit,' says the Lord of hosts." (Zechariah 4:6).

"But the Lord is faithful, and he will strengthen you and protect you from the evil one". *(2 Thessalonians 3:3).*

"Behold, I have given you authority to tread on serpents and scorpions, and over all the power of the enemy, and nothing shall hurt you." *(Luke 10:19).*

"The thief comes only to steal and kill and destroy. I came that they may have life and have it abundantly." *(John 10:10).*

"Truly I tell you, whatever you bind on earth will be bound in heaven, and whatever you loose on earth will be loosed in heaven. Again, truly I tell you that if two of you on earth agree about anything they ask for, it will be done for them by my Father in heaven." *(Matthew 18:18-19).*

"The Lord will cause your enemies who rise against you to be defeated before you. They shall come out against you one way and flee before you seven ways." *(Deuteronomy 28:7).*

"I have told you these things, so that in me you may have peace. In this world you will have trouble. But take heart! I have overcome the world." *(John 16:33).*

"No temptation has overtaken you except what is common to mankind. And God is faithful; he will not let you be tempted beyond what you can bear. But when you are tempted, he will also provide a way out so that you can endure it." *(1 Corinthians 10:13).*

"And you will know the truth, and the truth will set you free." *(John 8:32).*

"Do not be overcome with evil, but overcome evil with good." *(Romans 12:21).*

"And they have conquered him by the blood of the Lamb and by the word of their testimony, for they loved not their lives even unto death." *(Revelations 12:11)*.

"Fight the good fight of the faith. Take hold of the eternal life to which you were called when you made your good confession in the presence of many witnesses." *(1 Timothy 6:12)*.

"On this rock I will build my church, and the gates of hell shall not prevail against it." *(Matthew 16:8)*.

"…the reason the Son of God appeared was to destroy the devil's work." *(1 John 3:8)*.

"But they who wait for the Lord shall renew their strength; they shall mount up with wings like eagles; they shall run and not be weary; they shall walk and not faint." *(Isaiah 40:31)*.

"One of your men puts to flight a thousand, for the Lord your God is He who fights for you, just as He promised you." (*Joshua 23:10*).

"Do not fear them, for the Lord your God is the one fighting for you." *(Deuteronomy 3:22)*.

"What then shall we say to these things? If God is for us, who is against us?" *(Romans 8:31)*.

"Through You we will push back our adversaries, through Your name we will trample down those who rise up against us." *(Psalm 44:5)*.

"Have I not commanded you? Be strong and courageous! Do not tremble or be dismayed, for the Lord your God is with you wherever you go." *(Joshua 1:9)*.

"For You have girded me with strength for battle; You have subdued under me those who rose up against me." *(Psalm 18:39)*.

"He who dwells in the shelter of the Most High will rest in the shadow of the Almighty. I will say of the Lord, He is my refuge and my fortress, my God, in whom I trust. Surely, he will save you under his wings you will find refuge; his faithfulness will be your shield and rampart…" *(Psalms 91:1-4)*.

"This is what the Lord says to you: 'Do not be afraid or discouraged because of this vast army. For the battle is not yours, but God's." *(2 Chronicles 20:15)*.

The battle belongs to the Lord, and He has the final victory!

Cleanse Your Property of Demonic Influence

Many properties that have been previously lived in, and demonic interference in a home may come from spirits dwelling there before you moved in. This can include outside property areas as well. Demonic interference might be caused by others' actions, not yours. Therefore, now is the time to pray for the removal of any demonic force from your yard.

Remove Demonic Interference on Your Property

- Clear the Area:

    Remove trash, debris, or items that might harbor demonic forces—pagan symbols, statues, unknown objects, or clutter.

Renounce Sins

- "I renounce and ask forgiveness for sins that have defiled this land by anyone at any time, especially sins of Satanism, witchcraft, idolatry, bloodshed, immorality, and breaking covenants to You. Amen."

- "I renounce all ungodliness and sinful activity ever done in this home or land. I renounce the sins of previous owners, renters, guests, and builders. Any curses or evil covenants are broken and nullified in Jesus' name. In Jesus' name, I bind all demons here and command them to leave. I cancel enemy claims by the blood of Jesus Christ. Cleanse this home and all its contents in Jesus' name. Amen."

Prayers for Binding Demons

- "Lord Jesus, in Your holy name, I bind and forbid any demonic forces to manifest on this property. Remove all demons and attachments. Amen."

- "In Jesus' name, I bind all spirits in the air, fire, water, ground, and underground. I bind satanic forces of nature. I command all unclean spirits to leave now in Jesus' name. Amen."
- "Lord Jesus, I bind all spirits trying to take revenge on me, my family, friends, and community. I bind all evil spirits and satanic forces operating in the air, water, ground, fire, underground, or nature, and emissaries from satanic headquarters. By Your Precious Blood, I bind all demons' attributes, interactions, and deceitful plans. I break all bonds and ties. Amen."

Prayers for Protection Over Your Property

To pray for the protection of your yard from demons, focus on seeking God's power and presence, invoking angels, and rebuking evil influences. You can use prayers like the one from *(Exodus 90)*, asking God to establish a perimeter of protection around you and your loved ones, including your yard. *(Psalm 91)* also speaks of God's refuge and protection.

"Lord Jesus, in Your love and mercy, establish a perimeter of protection around my family, myself, and all our loved ones. I ask that the Holy Angels guard us, all our possessions, and this property, rendering us immune to any demonic influence. Let no demonic bondage, door, entity, portal, astral projection, or disembodied spirit enter this property in any direction. Send Your angels to protect us from harm, including demon interference within our property's vicinity. Prevent any demons from trying to enter by Your angels. Strip them of weapons and authority. Bind, rebuke, and disable their communication and interaction. Remove them to the Abyss. All this I ask in Your holy name. Amen."

"Heavenly Father, I come before You seeking Your guidance and protection for this home. Cleanse this space of negativity, darkness, and unholy influences. I command all evil spirits and forces to leave in Jesus' name. I invite Your Holy Spirit to fill this home with love, peace, and presence. I dedicate this house to You, Lord, and pray it may be a place of joy, healing, and blessing. Thank You for Your faithfulness and protection. Amen."

"Lord Jesus, You are the Head of this household. I invite Your authority and dominion to reign here. In Your powerful name, I bind every demon and cast them into the abyss. I command that no demonic forces operate or linger here. Amen."

"Heavenly Father, I ask Your presence and protection in this home. Cleanse it from evil influences and spiritual disturbances. Let Your holy light shine in every corner, filling this home with love and peace. Surround us and all who live here with divine protection. Guard us from harm, seen and unseen, and keep us safe from spiritual attacks. Bless this home and all who enter, that they may feel Your presence and peace. In Jesus' name, I command all demons to leave. Thank You, Jesus, for cleansing and purifying this home. Thank You, Lord, for Your presence and protection. Through the Holy Spirit and Your angels, may this home be a sanctuary of peace, love, and joy, where Your name is honored and Your will done. Amen."

Consecrate Your Home and Property to God

Consecration means separating anything unclean, especially that which would harm your relationship with God. It means sanctification, holiness, and purity. To consecrate is to dedicate or set apart yourself and your belongings for God's service and worship. It is a personal commitment to live a life holy and pleasing to God, often involving turning away from worldly pursuits and focusing on spiritual growth and service.

Consecration and Dedication Prayers

The prayer of consecration is where you dedicate yourself or something to God's purposes, setting it apart as holy. It is a deliberate surrender to God's will, aligning your life or possessions with His purposes. You dedicate your time, talents, or physical possessions to God's work.

Sample Prayer of Consecration:

Heavenly Father,

I now consecrate and dedicate this home and the land it sits on to the rule of Jesus, the presence of the Holy Spirit, and the Kingdom of God. I dedicate everything in and around this house to the Lord Jesus and claim it under His rule and protection. I ask Your blessing in every room and on everything within it. Come, Holy Spirit, fill every part of this home with the fullness of Your kingdom, love, peace, and rest. Jesus, send Your angels now to cleanse this home, establish Your kingdom, and build a shield of protection around it. In the mighty name of The Lord Jesus Christ, I proclaim this home, land, and all within it as property of the Kingdom of God. Amen

Ongoing Prayer Declarations:

- "Lord, I invite Your authority and dominion to reign over this place. Through Your name's power, I bind every spiritual enemy and cast them far from these premises. No demonic forces may operate or linger here. Establish Your kingdom rule and surround this home with angels for protection."

- "Come, Holy Spirit. Fill every part of this home with the fullness of Your kingdom, Your love, peace, and rest. Jesus, send Your angels to cleanse this home, establish Your kingdom here, and build a shield of protection. In Jesus Christ's mighty name, I proclaim this home, land, and all within as the Kingdom of God's property."

Spiritual Warfare Scriptures

The concept of "God reading the word" refers to the idea that God's Word, often understood as the Bible, is a living and active force, a source of divine truth and guidance, and a reflection of God's character and will.

"Submit yourselves to God. Resist the devil, and he will flee from you." *(James 4:7)*.

"You are from God, little children, and have overcome them; because greater is He who is in you than he who is in the world." *(1 John 4:4)*.

"For though we live in the world, we do not wage war as the world does. The weapons we fight with are not the weapons of the world. On the contrary, they have divine power to demolish strongholds. We demolish arguments and every pretension that sets itself up against the knowledge of God, and we take captive every thought to make it obedient to Christ." *(2 Corinthians 10:3-5)*.

"Be self-controlled and alert. Your enemy the devil prowls around like a roaring lion looking for someone to devour. Resist him, standing firm in the faith." *(1 Peter 5:8-9)*.

"No weapon that is formed against you will prosper; and every tongue that accuses you in judgment you will condemn. This is the heritage of the servants of the Lord, and their vindication is from Me," declares the Lord." *(Isaiah 54:17)*.

Put on the full armor of God, so that you can take your stand against the devil's schemes. For our struggle is not against flesh and blood, but against the rulers, against the authorities, against the powers of this dark world and against the spiritual forces of evil in the heavenly realms. Therefore put on the full armor of God, so that when the day of evil comes, you may be able to stand your ground, and after you have done everything, to stand. Stand firm then, with the belt of truth buckled around your waist, with the breastplate of righteousness in place, and with your feet fitted with the readiness that comes from the gospel of peace. In addition to all this, take up the shield of faith, with which you can extinguish all the flaming arrows of the evil one. Take the helmet of salvation and the sword of the Spirit, which is the word of God." *(Ephesians 6:11-17)*.

"In all these things, we are more than conquerors through Him who loved us." *(Romans 8:37)*.

"But thanks be to God, who gives us the victory through our Lord Jesus Christ" *(1 Corinthians 15:57)*.

"Not by might nor by power, but by My Spirit,' says the Lord of hosts." *(Zechariah 4:6)*.

"But the Lord is faithful, and he will strengthen you and protect you from the evil one". *(2 Thessalonians 3:3)*.

"Behold, I have given you authority to tread on serpents and scorpions, and over all the power of the enemy, and nothing shall hurt you." *(Luke 10:19)*.

"The thief comes only to steal and kill and destroy. I came that they may have life and have it abundantly." *(John 10:10)*.

"Truly I tell you, whatever you bind on earth will be bound in heaven, and whatever you loose on earth will be loosed in heaven. Again, truly I tell you that if two of you on earth agree about anything they ask for, it will be done for them by my Father in heaven." *(Matthew 18:18-19)*.

"The Lord will cause your enemies who rise against you to be defeated before you. They shall come out against you one way and flee before you seven ways." *(Deuteronomy 28:7)*.

"I have told you these things, so that in me you may have peace. In this world you will have trouble. But take heart! I have overcome the world." *(John 16:33)*.

"No temptation has overtaken you except what is common to mankind. And God is faithful; he will not let you be tempted beyond what you can bear. But when you are tempted, he will also provide a way out so that you can endure it." *(1 Corinthians 10:13).*

"And you will know the truth, and the truth will set you free." *(John 8:32).*

"Do not be overcome with evil, but overcome evil with good." *(Romans 12:21).*

"And they have conquered him by the blood of the Lamb and by the word of their testimony, for they loved not their lives even unto death." *(Revelations 12:11).*

"Fight the good fight of the faith. Take hold of the eternal life to which you were called when you made your good confession in the presence of many witnesses." *(1 Timothy 6:12).*

"On this rock I will build my church, and the gates of hell shall not prevail against it." *(Matthew 16:8).*

"...the reason the Son of God appeared was to destroy the devil's work." *(1 John 3:8).*

"But they who wait for the Lord shall renew their strength; they shall mount up with wings like eagles; they shall run and not be weary; they shall walk and not faint." *(Isaiah 40:31).*

"One of your men puts to flight a thousand, for the Lord your God is He who fights for you, just as He promised you." *(Joshua 23:10).*

"Do not fear them, for the Lord your God is the one fighting for you." *(Deuteronomy 3:22).*

"What then shall we say to these things? If God is for us, who is against us?" *(Romans. 8:31).*

"Through You we will push back our adversaries, through Your name we will trample down those who rise up against us." *(Psalm 44:5).*

"Have I not commanded you? Be strong and courageous! Do not tremble or be dismayed, for the Lord your God is with you wherever you go." *(Joshua 1:9)*.

"For You have girded me with strength for battle; You have subdued under me those who rose up against me." *(Psalm 18:39)*.

"He who dwells in the shelter of the Most High will rest in the shadow of the Almighty. I will say of the Lord, He is my refuge and my fortress, my God, in whom I trust. Surely, he will save you under his wings you will find refuge; his faithfulness will be your shield and rampart..." *(Psalms 91:1-4)*.

"This is what the Lord says to you: 'Do not be afraid or discouraged because of this vast army. For the battle is not yours, but God's." *(2 Chronicles 20:15)*.

The battle belongs to the Lord, and He has the final victory!

CHAPTER 9

Baptism and Your Children

Baptism and Deliverance Ministry

Baptism and Deliverance Ministry are related but different spiritual concepts.

Baptism represents cleansing from sin and a new beginning in Christ. It is a public declaration of faith, symbolizing God's grace for forgiveness of sin, new life in Christ, entrance into the Church, and eternal salvation for believers. It also brings the Holy Spirit living within us., along with spiritual gifts and union with Jesus. Baptism is a foundational step and represents spiritual cleansing from sin, but it does not directly address demonic influence or oppression.

Deliverance Ministry involves freedom from darkness, demonic influence, and sin. It provides a personal experience and is specifically aimed at addressing the impact of demonic forces on an individual's life. It focuses on casting out demons and breaking demonic oppression through spiritual warfare. Deliverance Ministry calls on the power of the name of Jesus and the Holy Spirit's guidance and protection.

Demonic possession is much harder. This is when demons have actually taken control of the person's body, mind, emotions, and soul. In many cases, without faith in Jesus, Baptism, and the power of the Holy Spirit, the best way to deal with demonic possession is through exorcism.

When you and your children have received a new life through baptism and the Holy Spirit living within, Satan's power is limited to influencing thoughts and emotions. Without baptism, Satan can fully control the mind, body, and emotions. His goal is to kill, steal, and destroy all mankind, including your children.

Baptism

John the Baptist contrasted his water baptism for sin's forgiveness with Jesus' baptism: "I baptize with water, but He will baptize you with the Holy Spirit." *(Mark 1:8) (John 1:33, Matthew 3:11, Luke 3:16)*.

Baptism publicly represents your relationship with Christ. It is a public declaration of faith in Jesus Christ as your Lord and Savior, a formal rejection of sin, and an act of obedience to Jesus's command. He commanded his followers to baptize believers in the name of the Father, Son, and Holy Spirit. It marks an individual's entrance into the Christian faith and introduction into the Christian life with a community of believers. Baptism brings the forgiveness of sins, a new spiritual life, and the gift of the Holy Spirit. It symbolizes a believer's identification with the death, burial, and resurrection of Jesus Christ, representing a new life in Christ.

Baptism Brings:

Symbol of New Life

Baptism symbolizes our identification with Jesus' death and resurrection, signifying a transformation and commitment to living a Christ-centered life. "We were therefore buried with him through baptism into death in order that, just as Christ was raised from the dead through the glory of the Father, we too may live a new life." *(Romans 6:4)*.

Public Declaration

It is a public declaration of faith, marking a believer's choice to follow Jesus and live in obedience to His teachings. "Therefore go and make disciples of all nations, baptizing them in the name of the Father and of the Son and of the Holy Spirit, and teaching them to obey everything I have commanded you. And surely I am with you always, to the very end of the age." *(Matthew 28:19-20)*.

Washing of Sins

Baptism is often understood as a washing away of sins and a cleansing of the soul. "Peter replied, "Repent and be baptized, every one of you, in the name of Jesus Christ for the forgiveness of your sins. And you will receive the gift of the Holy Spirit". (Acts 2:38).

Incorporation into the Body of Christ

Baptism unites believers into one body through the Holy Spirit, regardless of their previous distinctions. "For we were all baptized by one Spirit so as to form one body—whether Jews or Gentiles, slave or free—and we were all given the one Spirit to drink. *(1 Corinthians 12:13)*.

Water and the Holy Spirit

The Bible emphasizes the connection between water baptism and the baptism of the Holy Spirit, which empowers believers to live a new life. "For John baptized with water, but in a few days you will be baptized with the Holy Spirit." *(Acts 1:5)*. Peter replied, "Repent and be baptized, every one of you, in the name of Jesus Christ for the forgiveness of your sins. And you will receive the gift of the Holy Spirit." *(Acts 2:38)*.

Immersion

The most common understanding of baptism is immersion in water, symbolizing the burial and resurrection of Jesus." Or don't you know that all of us who were baptized into Christ Jesus were baptized into his death? We were therefore buried with him through baptism into death in order that, just Christ was raised from the dead through the glory of the Father, we too may live a new life. For if we have been united with him in a death like his, we will certainly also be united with him in a resurrection like his." *(Romans 6:3)*.

One Baptism

The Bible teaches that there is one baptism, referring to the baptism commanded by Jesus and the apostles. "There is one body and one Spirit, just as you were called to one hope when you were called; one Lord, one faith, one baptism; one God and Father of all, who is over all and through all and in all." *(Ephesians 4:4-6).*

The Presence of the Holy Spirit

Baptism in the Holy Spirit is an experience where believers are filled with the Holy Spirit, empowering them for Christian service and ministry. While some denominations emphasize a separate experience after conversion, others believe the Holy Spirit enters the believer upon Baptism. To be baptized in the Holy Spirit, a believer can pray, confessing their need for the Spirit and asking God to fill them. Faith and expectation are crucial, as is yielding to God's will.

The difference in your life and your children's lives is faith and the presence of the Holy Spirit. Demons can never fully succeed in taking over your life through oppression. The same temptations and evil thoughts may be presented by them, but God is on your side. Turn to Him in faith and He will help you through any bad time you or your children are experiencing. According to the Bible, our goal is to think rightly about demons, especially since their ultimate fear is the name of Jesus Christ.

"You believe that there is one God. Good! Even the demons believe that—and shudder" *(James 2:19).*

"If you love me, keep my commandments. And I will ask the Father, and he will give you another Helper, to be with you forever, even the Spirit of truth." *(John 14:15-17).*

"Do you not know that you are God's temple and that the Spirit of God dwells in you?" *(1 Corinthians 3:16).*

"For in one Spirit we were all baptized into one body—Jews or Greeks, slaves or free—and all have been given the same Spirit to drink." *(1 Corinthians 12:13).*

"For John baptized with water, but in a few days you will be baptized with the Holy Spirit." *(Acts 1:5).*

Baptizing Infants

Baptism is a sign of God's covenant with believers and their families, similar to circumcision in the Old Testament. Some Christians believe infant baptism initiates new life and conveys God's grace and forgiveness. They see infant baptism as a way to incorporate children into the faith community from a young age, ensuring they are raised in a Christian environment.

Christian Environment.

Baptism is a sign of God's covenant with believers and their families, similar to circumcision in the Old Testament. Some. Christians believe that baptism, especially for infants, initiates a new life and conveys God's grace and forgiveness. They see infant baptism as a way to incorporate children into the faith community from a young age, ensuring they are raised in a Christian environment.

Infant and young child baptism is a Christian practice where infants or young children are baptized, typically with water, signifying their inclusion into the faith community. In the New Testament, there is no record of infant baptism.

In Christianity, baptism is seen as a sacred ritual believed to affect the soul by symbolically washing away sins, granting a new spiritual life, and uniting the individual with God and the Christian community. Through baptism, individuals become children of God, enter into a relationship with Him, and receive a new spiritual life.

As early as the second century, By 354-430 AD, infant baptism was accepted as standard practice in Christianity. The early church came to understand that Baptism removes the guilt of original sin, inherited from Adam and Eve, and restores the soul to a state of being in God's favor, having a relationship of peace and communion with Him, freedom from the penalty of sin, and is empowered by

His grace. Infant baptism has been practiced by many Christian churches throughout history.

Today, Roman Catholics, most Orthodox churches, Lutherans, Anglicans, Episcopalians, Presbyterians, Reformed traditions, and Methodists practice infant baptism. Many see it as a sign of grace and a way to incorporate children into the church. Other Christian traditions support infant baptism because they understand baptism to be the New Covenant equivalent of circumcision. Just as circumcision joined Old Testament Hebrews to the Abrahamic and Mosaic covenants, baptism is believed to join a person to the New Covenant of salvation through Jesus Christ. This view is based on Paul's statement, "When you came to Christ, you were 'circumcised,' but not by a physical procedure. Christ performed a spiritual circumcision—the cutting away of your sinful nature. For you were buried with Christ when you were baptized. And with him you were raised to new life because you trusted the mighty power of God, who raised Christ from the dead" *(Colossians 2:11-12)*.

Churches that practice infant baptism believe that baptism is how a person receives the Holy Spirit. They base this belief on Peter's words, "Repent and be baptized, every one of you, in the name of Jesus Christ for the forgiveness of your sins. And you will receive the gift of the Holy Spirit." *(Acts 2:38)*. They believe baptism sets the child apart and secures salvation. Household baptisms in the New Testament are cited as evidence that whole families were saved and baptized (assuming that children and babies were included, and not just adults. *(Acts 11:14; 16:15, 18:8), (1 Corinthians 1:16)*. The practice of Infant Baptism in the Bible assumption goes beyond what the Bible says.

In today's church, there are two schools of thought about baptism. The churches that do not baptize infants or young children stand on the New Testament's repeated emphasis on repentance and faith in Christ. An infant cannot repent and place his or her faith in Christ. A newborn cannot understand the gospel and consciously decide to obey and submit to Jesus. Babies are oblivious to the spiritual significance of water baptism. They believe that baptism, being an act that follows committed belief in Jesus Christ, as their Lord and Savior, should only be performed on those who have chosen to believe in and follow Christ. Since the original word translated as "baptize" means "to dip or immerse in water," believer's baptism is usually done by total immersion. Churches that typically practice submersion baptism include Baptists, Church of Christ, and The Church of Jesus Christ of Latter-day Saints. Some Pentecostal denominations also utilize immersion baptism. Eastern Orthodox churches, which view baptism as an immersion only, also perform infant baptisms by submersion.

Other churches approve of Infant Baptism. They see it as a way to welcome children into the Christian faith and offer them the benefits of baptism, such as being cleansed from sin and receiving God's grace. They also see it as a public declaration of the parents' faith and a commitment to raise the child in the faith. Some argue that baptism is the beginning of a lifelong journey of faith, not the end, and that it is appropriate even for those who are not yet able to understand or speak their faith. Infant baptism typically involves sprinkling with water or pouring water over the forehead. The religious rite of sprinkling water onto a person's forehead or of immersion in water, symbolizes cleansing of sin and restoring a person's relationship with God. Also, a new spiritual life and admission to the Christian Church.

Some denominations baptize an infant and accompany Baptism with formally giving the child's name. This name is given before God, the Church, and the congregation, signifying the child's entry into Christian life and their new identity as a follower of Jesus.

All this being said, Infant and young child baptism is a decision for the parents and their church. If Christian parents wish to dedicate their child to Christ, a baby dedication service instead of baptism is also appropriate. There is no biblical mandate or example of baptizing a baby. Whether an infant is dedicated or baptized or both, he or she will, at some point in the future the child will still need to make a personal decision to repent of sin and trust in Jesus Christ for salvation.

Baptizing Young Children

Baptizing a young child centers around your child's open, personal, public declaration of faith in Jesus, obeying Christ's command, and formally committing to an ongoing life of faith. It is a step toward a deeper, personal, and spiritual understanding of salvation. It is also a commitment for you and your child to intentionally live a more Christian life.

In many denominations, the "Age of Reason" is around the age of seven, when your child is old enough to understand and make their own faith decision. This preparation usually includes a time of formal religious education so your child can learn more about what Baptism means and how it personally applies to them. This preparation may involve attending classes, studying scripture, and learning how Baptism applies to their life.

You, as a parent, play a crucial role in the preparation and baptism of your older child. You are expected to be an active participant in your child's religious formation and to support their faith journey. By modeling your own faith in your daily life, you show your child how to respond to life—whether in difficult situations, expressing trust in God, or seeking His guidance. Also, by living out your faith through acts of kindness, regular church attendance, or consistent prayer, your child is more likely to follow your lead.

Prayer

When you pray with your child—either as a family or individually—you show your child how prayer helps you during challenging times. By making prayer a regular part of your day, whether before meals, bedtime, or during times of need or celebration, you model the power of prayer. You also demonstrate that you care about their well-being when you pray for their academic achievements, relationships, or other concerns.

Church

Show your child the importance of the "community of believers" by regularly attending church as a family. Participate with your child in worship, fellowship, and other activities. Look for a church that offers age-appropriate programs and a welcoming environment for children. Encourage your child to get involved in youth groups, Sunday school, or other church activities.

Faith

Share your faith and how you came to believe in Jesus. Talk about the challenges you have faced and how your faith in God helped you grow. Sharing your faith journey makes faith more concrete and real for your child. Let your child know that they can also rely on their own faith to navigate their own challenges.

The Bible

Provide age-appropriate resources and support your child as they study the Bible. Create a safe space for them to ask questions, express doubts, and share their thoughts. Read the Bible together as a family so everyone has an opportunity to share their thoughts and feelings.

Celebrate

Celebrate significant moments in your child's faith journey, such as baptism or confirmation. Also, celebrate all types of successes, whether in church or outside of it. Celebrate their spiritual growth and understanding.

Support

You need to stay connected with other Christian parents. They can help you work through the concerns you have regarding your child or your own spiritual life. You can find groups or organizations inside or outside of the Church. These groups can walk with you in good times and help guide you through challenges. They can be an encouragement to you and your family.

Church Leaders

If you are struggling to help your child with their faith journey, reach out to pastors, youth leaders, and friends for support and guidance. Ask them how you can best support your child.

Godparents

A godparent, also known as a godfather or godmother, is a person chosen by you to help guide your child. Godparents play an important role in your child's faith development. They are expected to be positive role models, demonstrating strong faith and moral character. They are charged with supporting your child's spiritual development and assisting you in raising your child in the faith. This is also true in the secular world. Godparents are a source of support, advice, and positive influence for your child throughout their life—offering guidance, support, and encouragement.

Many non-liturgical and non-denominational churches focus on individual faith and may not have a formal role for godparents in baptism.

Confirmation

Confirmation usually happens around age 12. It is a Christian rite in many denominations. As a baptized child of about twelve years old, your child will have the opportunity to publicly reaffirm their baptismal vows and express a mature commitment to their faith. This is a significant step in your child's spiritual journey, often involving instruction in the faith and a ceremony with laying on of hands, anointing, and prayer. It is sometimes seen as the completion of Baptism for young children. Your child confirms personal responsibility for their faith and commits to strengthening their faith in God.

Baptizing of Teens

There is no universally accepted age for child baptism, as different Christian denominations have varying practices. For those who practice "believer's baptism," children are baptized upon professing their faith. Some churches consider your child ready to decide and be baptized once they reach an age of accountability, typically around seven to twelve years old. Others may wait until your child shows a more mature understanding of faith and the implications of baptism, which could be around 13 to 18 years old.

Baptizing children and teens centers around your child openly declaring faith and obedience to Christ's command. It is a public affirmation of their salvation, symbolizing their commitment to a life of faith and new life in Christ. Baptism is viewed as a step toward deeper spiritual understanding, a more intentional Christian life, and a commitment to follow Jesus. By being immersed in or sprinkled with water, Baptism symbolizes cleansing and new life in Christ.

Ways to Talk to Your Child About Baptism

You want your child to have a close relationship with God, Jesus, and the Holy Spirit. But sometimes it can be difficult to help your child understand and appreciate the significance of baptism and to come to the decision to be baptized. So, how can you talk to your child about baptism?

Understand Why They Are Choosing Baptism

Baptism serves as your child's public declaration of faith, expressing their commitment to Jesus and His teachings. It is important that your child understands the meaning of baptism, makes a conscious decision to be baptized, and chooses to follow Christ. Baptism visually represents being a "new creation" in Christ, signifying a transformation in your child's life. Before deciding on baptism, it is best for your child to reach an age of understanding and accountability so they fully grasp the implications of their choice. Many children and teens decide to be baptized after a personal encounter with God, recognizing their need for Him.

Why Children Choose to Be Baptized

Baptism is a confirmation of faith. It gives your child the opportunity to publicly confirm their faith and commit to following Jesus. It allows them to make a public statement about their faith and be accountable to their church community. Baptism is a significant step in your child's spiritual journey, marking a movement toward or transition into adulthood.

Do Not Force the Idea or Conversation

Like many parenting scenarios, your child will probably show signs when they are ready to talk about baptism. If your child recently trusted Jesus or is asking questions about faith, it could be a good time to bring up baptism. Ask if they understand what baptism is, if they have friends who have been baptized, and whether they are thinking about baptism for themselves. Sharing your own faith with them is very important. Equally important is allowing your child to share their faith with others.

Reading and talking about Bible resources together helps. Especially read about Jesus being baptized by John the Baptist in *(Matthew 3:13-17)*. Following your child's lead and discussing how Jesus has influenced their life is important, as is sharing how He has influenced yours—it creates a meaningful walk together in Christ.

Prepare yourself for this conversation by reviewing common questions about baptism. You can be a resource for your child and help them begin their new relationship with Christ. Baptism is an exciting step for your child but also a vulnerable one. If you have personally chosen to be baptized, be sure you know why you made that decision in your own faith journey. Share how you felt going through your baptism—the good and the challenging.

This time is one for reflection for both of you. Often personal stories arise—some happy, some sad, some difficult. Sharing the thoughts, feelings, and experiences that led your child to Jesus can be challenging. If your child is not interested in talking right now, praise them for sharing this good news about baptism with you, and remind them you are always available to talk.

Most importantly, avoid putting unnecessary pressure on your child to decide about baptism. As parents, you want what is best for your child and sometimes try to make things happen. But baptism is ultimately about their faith decision and their choice, not yours.

The "why" behind baptism can feel confusing for your child, especially with different churches having different approaches. When answering questions, keep your responses simple—do not get too complicated. Here are some key truths about baptism to remember when talking with your child:

Our Faith Is Meant to Be Shared

Baptism is a moment when, in front of your church family, your child affirms that Jesus is their rescuer and leader. Spiritually, baptism means that when believers are baptized into Christ Jesus, they are baptized into His death, signifying union with His death, burial, and resurrection. This implies a new life, free from the power of sin. "Or don't you know that all of us who were baptized into Christ Jesus were baptized into his death? We were therefore buried with him through baptism into death in order that, just as Christ was raised from the dead through the glory of the Father, we too may live a new life." *(Romans 6:3-4)*.

Opportunity to Encourage Your Child with Your Story

Your personal experiences, including struggles, may resonate with your child. This can inspire them to pursue a relationship with Jesus.

"Therefore, if anyone is in Christ, the new creation has come: The old has gone, the new is here!" *(2 Corinthians 5:17).*

"But in your hearts revere Christ as Lord. Always be prepared to give an answer to everyone who asks you to give the reason for the hope that you have. But do this with gentleness and respect." *(1 Peter 3:15).*

Jesus Set the Model for Baptism

Baptism vividly reminds your child that they are a "new creation" because of what God has done through Jesus.

"Then Jesus came from Galilee to the Jordan to be baptized by John. But John tried to deter him, saying, I need to be baptized by you, and do you come to me? Jesus replied, 'Let it be so now; it is proper for us to do this to fulfill all righteousness." Then John consented. As soon as Jesus was baptized, he went up out of the water. At that moment, heaven was opened, and he saw the Spirit of God descending like a dove and alighting on him. And a voice from heaven said, "This is my Son, whom I love; with him I am well pleased.'" *(Matthew 3:13-17).*

"Therefore go and make disciples of all nations, baptizing them in the name of the Father and of the Son and of the Holy Spirit." *(Matthew 28:19).*

"Jesus answered, 'I am the way, the truth, and the life. No one can come to the Father except through me.'" *(John 14:6).*

Remember What Baptism Is Really About

It cannot be overstated how important it is to ensure your child has the right understanding of baptism. An individual relationship with Jesus, love from Jesus, and security with Jesus is not contingent on baptism. The only requirement to reconcile with God is to believe in and trust Jesus as your Savior. "For God so loved the world that he gave his one and only Son, that whoever believes in him shall not perish but have eternal life." *(John 3:16)*.

Baptism is a symbolic, outward declaration of that inward reality—not a path to it. It is essential to ensure your child's desire to be baptized does not come from a sense of obligation or shame.

Baptism Does Not Save Us from Our Sins—Jesus Does

Baptism by the Holy Spirit

Being baptized by the Holy Spirit, or having the Holy Spirit dwell within you, is a core tenet of the Christian faith. It refers to the moment when God's Spirit comes to live inside you as a believer, marking a shift from being a follower to becoming a part of the body of Christ. This baptism is distinct from water baptism, which is an outward symbol of an inward commitment.

The Baptism of the Holy Spirit is defined as the moment when the Spirit of God places you into union with Christ and into union with other believers in the body of Christ. The Holy Spirit fills your mind with genuine understanding of truth, takes possession of your abilities, and imparts gifts that qualify you for service in the body of Christ.

- The Baptism of the Holy Spirit was predicted by John the Baptist: "I baptize you with water, but he will baptize you with the Holy Spirit." *(Mark 1:8)*.

- Jesus, before He ascended to heaven, said: "For John baptized with water, but in a few days you will be baptized with the Holy Spirit." *(Acts 1:5)*.

- This promise was fulfilled on the Day of Pentecost. For the first time, people were permanently indwelt by the Holy Spirit, and the church began. "Then the day of Pentecost came, and they were all together in one place. Suddenly, a sound like the blowing of a violent wind came from heaven and filled the whole house where they were sitting. They saw what seemed to be tongues of fire that separated and came to rest on each of them. All of them were filled with the Holy Spirit and began to speak in other tongues as the Spirit enabled them." *(Acts 2:1-4)*.

- The central passage about the baptism of the Holy Spirit says: "Just as a body, though one, has many parts, but all its many parts form one body, so it is with Christ. For we were all baptized by one Spirit so as to form one body—whether Jews or Gentiles, slave or free—and we were all given the one Spirit to drink." *(1 Corinthians 12:12-13)*.

The Key Aspects of Baptism of the Holy Spirit

Water baptism is a public declaration of your faith; the baptism of the Holy Spirit is an internal experience that empowers you. Baptism signifies your new identity as a child of God, part of the body of Christ, and equips you to serve others. *(Romans14:8) (1 Thessalonians 4:16) (Revelation 14:13)*.

The Holy Spirit is promised to live within you, empowering you to live a life that pleases God *(John 14:1*6-17) (1 Corinthians 3:16). The Holy Spirit empowers you to carry out the work of God, enabling you to witness and share the gospel *(1 Corinthians 12:4) (Acts 2:4) (Romans 12:6-8) (Acts 4:31)*.

Baptism by the Holy Spirit Provides

Sharing the Gospel

The Holy Spirit empowers your evangelism, enabling you to offer help and love as you share the words of God *(Romans 12:6-8) (Acts 4:31) (Matthew 28:18-20)*.

Guides and Strengthens You for Ministry

- The Holy Spirit provides wisdom, understanding, and power for you to help others *(Romans 8:26) (Acts 1:8)*.

- The Holy Spirit guides, teaches, comforts, and reminds you of the teachings of Jesus *(John 14:26) (John 16:5-7)*.

- The Holy Spirit's gifts given to you include wisdom, knowledge, faith, healing, miraculous powers, prophecy, distinguishing spirits, speaking in tongues, and interpretation of tongues.

- The Holy Spirit's Talents given to you include prophecy, serving, teaching, encouraging, giving, leadership, mercy, word of wisdom, word of knowledge, faith, healing, miraculous powers, discerning spirits, speaking in tongues, interpretation of tongues, reflecting the unity and diversity of the body of the Church.

"Children are a heritage from the Lord,

offspring a reward from Him." *(Psalm 127:3)*

www.ingramcontent.com/pod-product-compliance
Lightning Source LLC
Chambersburg PA
CBHW®61800070526
44586CB00023B/2644